Three Books of Poems

by

Edwin Arlington Robinson

The Children of the Night
The Three Taverns
and
The Man against the Sky

ISBN-13: 978-1523314621
ISBN-10: 1523314621

Contents

The Children of the Night 7

Three Quatrains 10

The World 11

An Old Story 12

Ballade of a Ship 13

Ballade by the Fire 14

Ballade of Broken Flutes 15

Ballade of Dead Friends 16

Her Eyes 17

Two Men 19

Villanelle of Change 20

John Evereldown 21

Luke Havergal 22

The House on the Hill 23

Richard Cory 24

Two Octaves 25

Calvary 26

Dear Friends 27

The Story of the Ashes and the Flame 28

For Some Poems by Matthew Arnold 29

Amaryllis 30

Kosmos 31

Zola 32

The Pity of the Leaves 33

Aaron Stark 34

The Garden 35

Cliff Klingenhagen 36

Charles Carville's Eyes 37

The Dead Village 38

Boston 39

Two Sonnets 40

The Clerks 42

Fleming Helphenstine 43

For a Book by Thomas Hardy 44

Thomas Hood 45
The Miracle 46
Horace to Leuconoe 47
Reuben Bright 48
The Altar 49
The Tavern 50
Sonnet 51
George Crabbe 52
Credo 53
On the Night of a Friend's Wedding 54
Sonnet 55
Verlaine 56
Sonnet 57
Supremacy 58
The Night Before 59
Walt Whitman 69
The Chorus of Old Men in "Aegeus" 70
The Wilderness 72
Octaves 74
Two Quatrains 82
Romance 83
The Torrent 84
L'Envoi 85
The Three Taverns 86
The Valley of the Shadow 86
The Wandering Jew 89
Neighbors 91
The Mill 92
The Dark Hills 93
The Three Taverns 94
Demos I 103
Demos II 104
The Flying Dutchman 105
Tact 106
On the Way 107
John Brown 117
The False Gods 123

Archibald's Example 124
London Bridge 125
Tasker Norcross 130
A Song at Shannon's 139
Souvenir 140
Discovery 141
Firelight 142
The New Tenants 143
Inferential 144
The Rat 145
Rahel to Varnhagen 146
Nimmo 153
Peace on Earth 156
Late Summer 159
An Evangelist's Wife 162
The Old King's New Jester 163
Lazarus 165
The Man against the Sky 174
Flammonde 174
The Gift of God 178
The Clinging Vine 179
Cassandra 182
John Gorham 184
Stafford's Cabin 186
Hillcrest 187
Old King Cole 189
Ben Jonson Entertains a Man from Stratford 192
Eros Turannos 203
Old Trails 204
The Unforgiven 209
Theophilus 211
Veteran Sirens 212
Siege Perilous 213
Another Dark Lady 214
The Voice of Age 215
The Dark House 216
The Poor Relation 218

The Burning Book 220
Fragment 222
Lisette and Eileen 222
Llewellyn and the Tree 224
Bewick Finzer 228
Bokardo 229
The Man against the Sky 232
Index of First Lines 241

The Children of the Night
by
Edwin Arlington Robinson

[Maine Poet — 1869-1935.]

The Children of the Night

A Book of Poems by Edwin Arlington Robinson

To the Memory of my Father and Mother

The Children of the Night

For those that never know the light,
 The darkness is a sullen thing;
And they, the Children of the Night,
 Seem lost in Fortune's winnowing.

But some are strong and some are weak, —
 And there's the story. House and home
Are shut from countless hearts that seek
 World-refuge that will never come.

And if there be no other life,
 And if there be no other chance
To weigh their sorrow and their strife
 Than in the scales of circumstance,

'T were better, ere the sun go down
 Upon the first day we embark,
In life's imbittered sea to drown,
 Than sail forever in the dark.

But if there be a soul on earth
 So blinded with its own misuse
Of man's revealed, incessant worth,
 Or worn with anguish, that it views

No light but for a mortal eye,
 No rest but of a mortal sleep,
No God but in a prophet's lie,
 No faith for "honest doubt" to keep;

If there be nothing, good or bad,
 But chaos for a soul to trust, —
God counts it for a soul gone mad,
 And if God be God, He is just.

And if God be God, He is Love;
 And though the Dawn be still so dim,
It shows us we have played enough
 With creeds that make a fiend of Him.

There is one creed, and only one,
 That glorifies God's excellence;
So cherish, that His will be done,
 The common creed of common sense.

It is the crimson, not the gray,
 That charms the twilight of all time;
It is the promise of the day
 That makes the starry sky sublime;

It is the faith within the fear
 That holds us to the life we curse; —
So let us in ourselves revere
 The Self which is the Universe!

Let us, the Children of the Night,
 Put off the cloak that hides the scar!
Let us be Children of the Light,
 And tell the ages what we are!

Three Quatrains

I

As long as Fame's imperious music rings
 Will poets mock it with crowned words august;
And haggard men will clamber to be kings
 As long as Glory weighs itself in dust.

II

Drink to the splendor of the unfulfilled,
 Nor shudder for the revels that are done:
The wines that flushed Lucullus are all spilled,
 The strings that Nero fingered are all gone.

III

We cannot crown ourselves with everything,
 Nor can we coax the Fates for us to quarrel:
No matter what we are, or what we sing,
 Time finds a withered leaf in every laurel.

The World

Some are the brothers of all humankind,
 And own them, whatsoever their estate;
And some, for sorrow and self-scorn, are blind
 With enmity for man's unguarded fate.

For some there is a music all day long
 Like flutes in Paradise, they are so glad;
And there is hell's eternal under-song
 Of curses and the cries of men gone mad.

Some say the Scheme with love stands luminous,
 Some say 't were better back to chaos hurled;
And so 't is what we are that makes for us
 The measure and the meaning of the world.

An Old Story

Strange that I did not know him then,
 That friend of mine!
I did not even show him then
 One friendly sign;

But cursed him for the ways he had
 To make me see
My envy of the praise he had
 For praising me.

I would have rid the earth of him
 Once, in my pride! …
I never knew the worth of him
 Until he died.

Ballade of a Ship

Down by the flash of the restless water
 The dim White Ship like a white bird lay;
Laughing at life and the world they sought her,
 And out she swung to the silvering bay.
 Then off they flew on their roystering way,
And the keen moon fired the light foam flying
 Up from the flood where the faint stars play,
And the bones of the brave in the wave are lying.

'T was a king's fair son with a king's fair daughter,
 And full three hundred beside, they say, —
Revelling on for the lone, cold slaughter
 So soon to seize them and hide them for aye;
 But they danced and they drank and their souls grew gay,
Nor ever they knew of a ghoul's eye spying
 Their splendor a flickering phantom to stray
Where the bones of the brave in the wave are lying.

Through the mist of a drunken dream they brought her
 (This wild white bird) for the sea-fiend's prey:
The pitiless reef in his hard clutch caught her,
 And hurled her down where the dead men stay.
 A torturing silence of wan dismay —
Shrieks and curses of mad souls dying —
 Then down they sank to slumber and sway
Where the bones of the brave in the wave are lying.

ENVOY

Prince, do you sleep to the sound alway
 Of the mournful surge and the sea-birds' crying? —
Or does love still shudder and steel still slay,
 Where the bones of the brave in the wave are lying?

Ballade by the Fire

Slowly I smoke and hug my knee,
 The while a witless masquerade
Of things that only children see
 Floats in a mist of light and shade:
 They pass, a flimsy cavalcade,
And with a weak, remindful glow,
 The falling embers break and fade,
As one by one the phantoms go.

Then, with a melancholy glee
 To think where once my fancy strayed,
I muse on what the years may be
 Whose coming tales are all unsaid,
 Till tongs and shovel, snugly laid
Within their shadowed niches, grow
 By grim degrees to pick and spade,
As one by one the phantoms go.

But then, what though the mystic Three
 Around me ply their merry trade? —
And Charon soon may carry me
 Across the gloomy Stygian glade? —
 Be up, my soul! nor be afraid
Of what some unborn year may show;
 But mind your human debts are paid,
As one by one the phantoms go.

ENVOY

Life is the game that must be played:
 This truth at least, good friend, we know;
So live and laugh, nor be dismayed
 As one by one the phantoms go.

Ballade of Broken Flutes

(To A. T. Schumann.)

In dreams I crossed a barren land,
 A land of ruin, far away;
Around me hung on every hand
 A deathful stillness of decay;
 And silent, as in bleak dismay
That song should thus forsaken be,
 On that forgotten ground there lay
The broken flutes of Arcady.

The forest that was all so grand
 When pipes and tabors had their sway
Stood leafless now, a ghostly band
 Of skeletons in cold array.
 A lonely surge of ancient spray
Told of an unforgetful sea,
 But iron blows had hushed for aye
The broken flutes of Arcady.

No more by summer breezes fanned,
 The place was desolate and gray;
But still my dream was to command
 New life into that shrunken clay.
 I tried it. Yes, you scan to-day,
With uncommiserating glee,
 The songs of one who strove to play
The broken flutes of Arcady.

ENVOY

So, Rock, I join the common fray,
 To fight where Mammon may decree;
And leave, to crumble as they may,
 The broken flutes of Arcady.

Ballade of Dead Friends

As we the withered ferns
 By the roadway lying,
Time, the jester, spurns
 All our prayers and prying —
 All our tears and sighing,
Sorrow, change, and woe —
 All our where-and-whying
For friends that come and go.

Life awakes and burns,
 Age and death defying,
Till at last it learns
 All but Love is dying;
 Love's the trade we're plying,
God has willed it so;
 Shrouds are what we're buying
For friends that come and go.

Man forever yearns
 For the thing that's flying.
Everywhere he turns,
 Men to dust are drying, —
 Dust that wanders, eying
(With eyes that hardly glow)
 New faces, dimly spying
For friends that come and go.

ENVOY

And thus we all are nighing
 The truth we fear to know:
Death will end our crying
 For friends that come and go.

16

Her Eyes

Up from the street and the crowds that went,
  Morning and midnight, to and fro,
Still was the room where his days he spent,
  And the stars were bleak, and the nights were slow.

Year after year, with his dream shut fast,
  He suffered and strove till his eyes were dim,
For the love that his brushes had earned at last, —
  And the whole world rang with the praise of him.

But he cloaked his triumph, and searched, instead,
  Till his cheeks were sere and his hairs were gray.
"There are women enough, God knows," he said. . . .
  "There are stars enough — when the sun's away."

Then he went back to the same still room
  That had held his dream in the long ago,
When he buried his days in a nameless tomb,
  And the stars were bleak, and the nights were slow.

And a passionate humor seized him there —
  Seized him and held him until there grew
Like life on his canvas, glowing and fair,
  A perilous face — and an angel's, too.

Angel and maiden, and all in one, —
  All but the eyes. — They were there, but yet
They seemed somehow like a soul half done.
  What was the matter? Did God forget? . . .

But he wrought them at last with a skill so sure
  That her eyes were the eyes of a deathless woman, —
With a gleam of heaven to make them pure,
  And a glimmer of hell to make them human.

17

God never forgets. — And he worships her
 There in that same still room of his,
For his wife, and his constant arbiter
 Of the world that was and the world that is.

And he wonders yet what her love could be
 To punish him after that strife so grim;
But the longer he lives with her eyes to see,
 The plainer it all comes back to him.

Two Men

There be two men of all mankind
  That I should like to know about;
But search and question where I will,
  I cannot ever find them out.

Melchizedek he praised the Lord,
  And gave some wine to Abraham;
But who can tell what else he did
  Must be more learned than I am.

Ucalegon he lost his house
  When Agamemnon came to Troy;
But who can tell me who he was —
  I'll pray the gods to give him joy.

There be two men of all mankind
  That I'm forever thinking on:
They chase me everywhere I go, —
  Melchizedek, Ucalegon.

Villanelle of Change

Since Persia fell at Marathon,
 The yellow years have gathered fast:
Long centuries have come and gone.

And yet (they say) the place will don
 A phantom fury of the past,
Since Persia fell at Marathon;

And as of old, when Helicon
 Trembled and swayed with rapture vast
(Long centuries have come and gone),

This ancient plain, when night comes on,
 Shakes to a ghostly battle-blast,
Since Persia fell at Marathon.

But into soundless Acheron
 The glory of Greek shame was cast:
Long centuries have come and gone,

The suns of Hellas have all shone,
 The first has fallen to the last: —
Since Persia fell at Marathon,
Long centuries have come and gone.

John Evereldown

"Where are you going to-night, to-night, —
 Where are you going, John Evereldown?
There's never the sign of a star in sight,
 Nor a lamp that's nearer than Tilbury Town.
Why do you stare as a dead man might?
Where are you pointing away from the light?
And where are you going to-night, to-night, —
 Where are you going, John Evereldown?"

"Right through the forest, where none can see,
 There's where I'm going, to Tilbury Town.
The men are asleep, — or awake, may be, —
 But the women are calling John Evereldown.
Ever and ever they call for me,
And while they call can a man be free?
So right through the forest, where none can see,
 There's where I'm going, to Tilbury Town."

"But why are you going so late, so late, —
 Why are you going, John Evereldown?
Though the road be smooth and the path be straight,
 There are two long leagues to Tilbury Town.
Come in by the fire, old man, and wait!
Why do you chatter out there by the gate?
And why are you going so late, so late, —
 Why are you going, John Evereldown?"

"I follow the women wherever they call, —
 That's why I'm going to Tilbury Town.
God knows if I pray to be done with it all,
 But God is no friend to John Evereldown.
So the clouds may come and the rain may fall,
The shadows may creep and the dead men crawl, —
But I follow the women wherever they call,
 And that's why I'm going to Tilbury Town."

Luke Havergal

Go to the western gate, Luke Havergal, —
There where the vines cling crimson on the wall, —
And in the twilight wait for what will come.
The wind will moan, the leaves will whisper some —
Whisper of her, and strike you as they fall;
But go, and if you trust her she will call.
Go to the western gate, Luke Havergal —
Luke Havergal.

No, there is not a dawn in eastern skies
To rift the fiery night that's in your eyes;
But there, where western glooms are gathering,
The dark will end the dark, if anything:
God slays Himself with every leaf that flies,
And hell is more than half of paradise.
No, there is not a dawn in eastern skies —
In eastern skies.

Out of a grave I come to tell you this, —
Out of a grave I come to quench the kiss
That flames upon your forehead with a glow
That blinds you to the way that you must go.
Yes, there is yet one way to where she is, —
Bitter, but one that faith can never miss.
Out of a grave I come to tell you this —
To tell you this.

There is the western gate, Luke Havergal,
There are the crimson leaves upon the wall.
Go, — for the winds are tearing them away, —
Nor think to riddle the dead words they say,
Nor any more to feel them as they fall;
But go! and if you trust her she will call.
There is the western gate, Luke Havergal —
Luke Havergal.

The House on the Hill

They are all gone away,
 The House is shut and still,
There is nothing more to say.

Through broken walls and gray
 The winds blow bleak and shrill:
They are all gone away.

Nor is there one to-day
 To speak them good or ill:
There is nothing more to say.

Why is it then we stray
 Around that sunken sill?
They are all gone away,

And our poor fancy-play
 For them is wasted skill:
There is nothing more to say.

There is ruin and decay
 In the House on the Hill:
They are all gone away,
There is nothing more to say.

Richard Cory

Whenever Richard Cory went down town,
We people on the pavement looked at him:
He was a gentleman from sole to crown,
Clean favored, and imperially slim.

And he was always quietly arrayed,
And he was always human when he talked;
But still he fluttered pulses when he said,
"Good-morning," and he glittered when he walked.

And he was rich, — yes, richer than a king, —
And admirably schooled in every grace:
In fine, we thought that he was everything
To make us wish that we were in his place.

So on we worked, and waited for the light,
And went without the meat, and cursed the bread;
And Richard Cory, one calm summer night,
Went home and put a bullet through his head.

Two Octaves

I

Not by the grief that stuns and overwhelms
All outward recognition of revealed
And righteous omnipresence are the days
Of most of us affrighted and diseased,
But rather by the common snarls of life
That come to test us and to strengthen us
In this the prentice-age of discontent,
Rebelliousness, faint-heartedness, and shame.

II

When through hot fog the fulgid sun looks down
Upon a stagnant earth where listless men
Laboriously dawdle, curse, and sweat,
Disqualified, unsatisfied, inert, —
It seems to me somehow that God himself
Scans with a close reproach what I have done,
Counts with an unphrased patience my arrears,
And fathoms my unprofitable thoughts.

Calvary

Friendless and faint, with martyred steps and slow,
Faint for the flesh, but for the spirit free,
Stung by the mob that came to see the show,
The Master toiled along to Calvary;
We gibed him, as he went, with houndish glee,
Till his dimmed eyes for us did overflow;
We cursed his vengeless hands thrice wretchedly, —
And this was nineteen hundred years ago.

But after nineteen hundred years the shame
Still clings, and we have not made good the loss
That outraged faith has entered in his name.
Ah, when shall come love's courage to be strong!
Tell me, O Lord — tell me, O Lord, how long
Are we to keep Christ writhing on the cross!

Dear Friends

Dear friends, reproach me not for what I do,
Nor counsel me, nor pity me; nor say
That I am wearing half my life away
For bubble-work that only fools pursue.
And if my bubbles be too small for you,
Blow bigger then your own: the games we play
To fill the frittered minutes of a day,
Good glasses are to read the spirit through.

And whoso reads may get him some shrewd skill;
And some unprofitable scorn resign,
To praise the very thing that he deplores;
So, friends (dear friends), remember, if you will,
The shame I win for singing is all mine,
The gold I miss for dreaming is all yours.

The Story of the Ashes and the Flame

No matter why, nor whence, nor when she came,
There was her place. No matter what men said,
No matter what she was; living or dead,
Faithful or not, he loved her all the same.
The story was as old as human shame,
But ever since that lonely night she fled,
With books to blind him, he had only read
The story of the ashes and the flame.

There she was always coming pretty soon
To fool him back, with penitent scared eyes
That had in them the laughter of the moon
For baffled lovers, and to make him think —
Before she gave him time enough to wink —
Sin's kisses were the keys to Paradise.

For Some Poems by Matthew Arnold

Sweeping the chords of Hellas with firm hand,
He wakes lost echoes from song's classic shore,
And brings their crystal cadence back once more
To touch the clouds and sorrows of a land
Where God's truth, cramped and fettered with a band
Of iron creeds, he cheers with golden lore
Of heroes and the men that long before
Wrought the romance of ages yet unscanned.

Still does a cry through sad Valhalla go
For Balder, pierced with Lok's unhappy spray —
For Balder, all but spared by Frea's charms;
And still does art's imperial vista show,
On the hushed sands of Oxus, far away,
Young Sohrab dying in his father's arms.

Amaryllis

Once, when I wandered in the woods alone,
An old man tottered up to me and said,
"Come, friend, and see the grave that I have made
For Amaryllis." There was in the tone
Of his complaint such quaver and such moan
That I took pity on him and obeyed,
And long stood looking where his hands had laid
An ancient woman, shrunk to skin and bone.

Far out beyond the forest I could hear
The calling of loud progress, and the bold
Incessant scream of commerce ringing clear;
But though the trumpets of the world were glad,
It made me lonely and it made me sad
To think that Amaryllis had grown old.

Kosmos

Ah, — shuddering men that falter and shrink so
To look on death, — what were the days we live,
Where life is half a struggle to forgive,
But for the love that finds us when we go?
Is God a jester? Does he laugh and throw
Poor branded wretches here to sweat and strive
For some vague end that never shall arrive?
And is He not yet weary of the show?

Think of it, all ye millions that have planned,
And only planned, the largess of hard youth!
Think of it, all ye builders on the sand,
Whose works are down! — Is love so small, forsooth?
Be brave! To-morrow you will understand
The doubt, the pain, the triumph, and the Truth!

Zola

Because he puts the compromising chart
Of hell before your eyes, you are afraid;
Because he counts the price that you have paid
For innocence, and counts it from the start,
You loathe him. But he sees the human heart
Of God meanwhile, and in God's hand has weighed
Your squeamish and emasculate crusade
Against the grim dominion of his art.

Never until we conquer the uncouth
Connivings of our shamed indifference
(We call it Christian faith!) are we to scan
The racked and shrieking hideousness of Truth
To find, in hate's polluted self-defence
Throbbing, the pulse, the divine heart of man.

The Pity of the Leaves

Vengeful across the cold November moors,
Loud with ancestral shame there came the bleak
Sad wind that shrieked, and answered with a shriek,
Reverberant through lonely corridors.
The old man heard it; and he heard, perforce,
Words out of lips that were no more to speak —
Words of the past that shook the old man's cheek
Like dead, remembered footsteps on old floors.

And then there were the leaves that plagued him so!
The brown, thin leaves that on the stones outside
Skipped with a freezing whisper. Now and then
They stopped, and stayed there — just to let him know
How dead they were; but if the old man cried,
They fluttered off like withered souls of men.

Aaron Stark

Withal a meagre man was Aaron Stark, —
Cursed and unkempt, shrewd, shrivelled, and morose.
A miser was he, with a miser's nose,
And eyes like little dollars in the dark.
His thin, pinched mouth was nothing but a mark;
And when he spoke there came like sullen blows
Through scattered fangs a few snarled words and close,
As if a cur were chary of its bark.

Glad for the murmur of his hard renown,
Year after year he shambled through the town, —
A loveless exile moving with a staff;
And oftentimes there crept into his ears
A sound of alien pity, touched with tears, —
And then (and only then) did Aaron laugh.

The Garden

There is a fenceless garden overgrown
With buds and blossoms and all sorts of leaves;
And once, among the roses and the sheaves,
The Gardener and I were there alone.
He led me to the plot where I had thrown
The fennel of my days on wasted ground,
And in that riot of sad weeds I found
The fruitage of a life that was my own.

My life! Ah, yes, there was my life, indeed!
And there were all the lives of humankind;
And they were like a book that I could read,
Whose every leaf, miraculously signed,
Outrolled itself from Thought's eternal seed,
Love-rooted in God's garden of the mind.

Cliff Klingenhagen

Cliff Klingenhagen had me in to dine
With him one day; and after soup and meat,
And all the other things there were to eat,
Cliff took two glasses and filled one with wine
And one with wormwood. Then, without a sign
For me to choose at all, he took the draught
Of bitterness himself, and lightly quaffed
It off, and said the other one was mine.

And when I asked him what the deuce he meant
By doing that, he only looked at me
And grinned, and said it was a way of his.
And though I know the fellow, I have spent
Long time a-wondering when I shall be
As happy as Cliff Klingenhagen is.

Charles Carville's Eyes

A melancholy face Charles Carville had,
But not so melancholy as it seemed, —
When once you knew him, — for his mouth redeemed
His insufficient eyes, forever sad:
In them there was no life-glimpse, good or bad, —
Nor joy nor passion in them ever gleamed;
His mouth was all of him that ever beamed,
His eyes were sorry, but his mouth was glad.

He never was a fellow that said much,
And half of what he did say was not heard
By many of us: we were out of touch
With all his whims and all his theories
Till he was dead, so those blank eyes of his
Might speak them. Then we heard them, every word.

The Dead Village

Here there is death. But even here, they say, —
Here where the dull sun shines this afternoon
As desolate as ever the dead moon
Did glimmer on dead Sardis, — men were gay;
And there were little children here to play,
With small soft hands that once did keep in tune
The strings that stretch from heaven, till too soon
The change came, and the music passed away.

Now there is nothing but the ghosts of things, —
No life, no love, no children, and no men;
And over the forgotten place there clings
The strange and unrememberable light
That is in dreams. The music failed, and then
God frowned, and shut the village from His sight.

Boston

My northern pines are good enough for me,
But there's a town my memory uprears —
A town that always like a friend appears,
And always in the sunrise by the sea.
And over it, somehow, there seems to be
A downward flash of something new and fierce,
That ever strives to clear, but never clears
The dimness of a charmed antiquity.

Two Sonnets

I

Just as I wonder at the twofold screen
Of twisted innocence that you would plait
For eyes that uncourageously await
The coming of a kingdom that has been,
So do I wonder what God's love can mean
To you that all so strangely estimate
The purpose and the consequent estate
Of one short shuddering step to the Unseen.

No, I have not your backward faith to shrink
Lone-faring from the doorway of God's home
To find Him in the names of buried men;
Nor your ingenious recreance to think
We cherish, in the life that is to come,
The scattered features of dead friends again.

II

Never until our souls are strong enough
To plunge into the crater of the Scheme —
Triumphant in the flash there to redeem
Love's handsel and forevermore to slough,
Like cerements at a played-out masque, the rough
And reptile skins of us whereon we set
The stigma of scared years — are we to get
Where atoms and the ages are one stuff.

Nor ever shall we know the cursed waste
Of life in the beneficence divine
Of starlight and of sunlight and soul-shine
That we have squandered in sin's frail distress,
Till we have drunk, and trembled at the taste,
The mead of Thought's prophetic endlessness.

The Clerks

I did not think that I should find them there
When I came back again; but there they stood,
As in the days they dreamed of when young blood
Was in their cheeks and women called them fair.
Be sure, they met me with an ancient air, —
And yes, there was a shop-worn brotherhood
About them; but the men were just as good,
And just as human as they ever were.

And you that ache so much to be sublime,
And you that feed yourselves with your descent,
What comes of all your visions and your fears?
Poets and kings are but the clerks of Time,
Tiering the same dull webs of discontent,
Clipping the same sad alnage of the years.

Fleming Helphenstine

At first I thought there was a superfine
Persuasion in his face; but the free glow
That filled it when he stopped and cried, "Hollo!"
Shone joyously, and so I let it shine.
He said his name was Fleming Helphenstine,
But be that as it may; — I only know
He talked of this and that and So-and-So,
And laughed and chaffed like any friend of mine.

But soon, with a queer, quick frown, he looked at me,
And I looked hard at him; and there we gazed
With a strained shame that made us cringe and wince:
Then, with a wordless clogged apology
That sounded half confused and half amazed,
He dodged, — and I have never seen him since.

For a Book by Thomas Hardy

With searching feet, through dark circuitous ways,
I plunged and stumbled; round me, far and near,
Quaint hordes of eyeless phantoms did appear,
Twisting and turning in a bootless chase, —
When, like an exile given by God's grace
To feel once more a human atmosphere,
I caught the world's first murmur, large and clear,
Flung from a singing river's endless race.

Then, through a magic twilight from below,
I heard its grand sad song as in a dream:
Life's wild infinity of mirth and woe
It sang me; and, with many a changing gleam,
Across the music of its onward flow
I saw the cottage lights of Wessex beam.

Thomas Hood

The man who cloaked his bitterness within
This winding-sheet of puns and pleasantries,
God never gave to look with common eyes
Upon a world of anguish and of sin:
His brother was the branded man of Lynn;
And there are woven with his jollities
The nameless and eternal tragedies
That render hope and hopelessness akin.

We laugh, and crown him; but anon we feel
A still chord sorrow-swept, — a weird unrest;
And thin dim shadows home to midnight steal,
As if the very ghost of mirth were dead —
As if the joys of time to dreams had fled,
Or sailed away with Ines to the West.

The Miracle

"Dear brother, dearest friend, when I am dead,
And you shall see no more this face of mine,
Let nothing but red roses be the sign
Of the white life I lost for him," she said;
"No, do not curse him, — pity him instead;
Forgive him! — forgive me! … God's anodyne

For human hate is pity; and the wine
That makes men wise, forgiveness. I have read
Love's message in love's murder, and I die."
And so they laid her just where she would lie, —
Under red roses. Red they bloomed and fell;
But when flushed autumn and the snows went by,
And spring came, — lo, from every bud's green shell
Burst a white blossom. — Can love reason why?

Horace to Leuconoe

I pray you not, Leuconoe, to pore
With unpermitted eyes on what may be
Appointed by the gods for you and me,
Nor on Chaldean figures any more.
'T were infinitely better to implore
The present only: — whether Jove decree
More winters yet to come, or whether he
Make even this, whose hard, wave-eaten shore
Shatters the Tuscan seas to-day, the last —
Be wise withal, and rack your wine, nor fill
Your bosom with large hopes; for while I sing,
The envious close of time is narrowing; —
So seize the day, — or ever it be past, —
And let the morrow come for what it will.

Reuben Bright

Because he was a butcher and thereby
Did earn an honest living (and did right),
I would not have you think that Reuben Bright
Was any more a brute than you or I;
For when they told him that his wife must die,
He stared at them, and shook with grief and fright,
And cried like a great baby half that night,
And made the women cry to see him cry.

And after she was dead, and he had paid
The singers and the sexton and the rest,
He packed a lot of things that she had made
Most mournfully away in an old chest
Of hers, and put some chopped-up cedar boughs
In with them, and tore down the slaughter-house.

The Altar

Alone, remote, nor witting where I went,
I found an altar builded in a dream —
A fiery place, whereof there was a gleam
So swift, so searching, and so eloquent
Of upward promise, that love's murmur, blent
With sorrow's warning, gave but a supreme
Unending impulse to that human stream
Whose flood was all for the flame's fury bent.

Alas! I said, — the world is in the wrong.
But the same quenchless fever of unrest
That thrilled the foremost of that martyred throng
Thrilled me, and I awoke ... and was the same
Bewildered insect plunging for the flame
That burns, and must burn somehow for the best.

The Tavern

Whenever I go by there nowadays
And look at the rank weeds and the strange grass,
The torn blue curtains and the broken glass,
I seem to be afraid of the old place;
And something stiffens up and down my face,
For all the world as if I saw the ghost
Of old Ham Amory, the murdered host,
With his dead eyes turned on me all aglaze.

The Tavern has a story, but no man
Can tell us what it is. We only know
That once long after midnight, years ago,
A stranger galloped up from Tilbury Town,
Who brushed, and scared, and all but overran
That skirt-crazed reprobate, John Evereldown.

Sonnet

Oh for a poet — for a beacon bright
To rift this changeless glimmer of dead gray;
To spirit back the Muses, long astray,
And flush Parnassus with a newer light;
To put these little sonnet-men to flight
Who fashion, in a shrewd, mechanic way,
Songs without souls, that flicker for a day,
To vanish in irrevocable night.

What does it mean, this barren age of ours?
Here are the men, the women, and the flowers,
The seasons, and the sunset, as before.
What does it mean? Shall not one bard arise
To wrench one banner from the western skies,
And mark it with his name forevermore?

George Crabbe

Give him the darkest inch your shelf allows,
Hide him in lonely garrets, if you will, —
But his hard, human pulse is throbbing still
With the sure strength that fearless truth endows.
In spite of all fine science disavows,
Of his plain excellence and stubborn skill
There yet remains what fashion cannot kill,
Though years have thinned the laurel from his brows.

Whether or not we read him, we can feel
From time to time the vigor of his name
Against us like a finger for the shame
And emptiness of what our souls reveal
In books that are as altars where we kneel
To consecrate the flicker, not the flame.

Credo

I cannot find my way: there is no star
In all the shrouded heavens anywhere;
And there is not a whisper in the air
Of any living voice but one so far
That I can hear it only as a bar
Of lost, imperial music, played when fair
And angel fingers wove, and unaware,
Dead leaves to garlands where no roses are.

No, there is not a glimmer, nor a call,
For one that welcomes, welcomes when he fears,
The black and awful chaos of the night;
For through it all, — above, beyond it all, —
I know the far-sent message of the years,
I feel the coming glory of the Light!

On the Night of a Friend's Wedding

If ever I am old, and all alone,
I shall have killed one grief, at any rate;
For then, thank God, I shall not have to wait
Much longer for the sheaves that I have sown.
The devil only knows what I have done,
But here I am, and here are six or eight
Good friends, who most ingenuously prate
About my songs to such and such a one.

But everything is all askew to-night, —
As if the time were come, or almost come,
For their untenanted mirage of me
To lose itself and crumble out of sight,
Like a tall ship that floats above the foam
A little while, and then breaks utterly.

Sonnet

The master and the slave go hand in hand,
Though touch be lost. The poet is a slave,
And there be kings do sorrowfully crave
The joyance that a scullion may command.
But, ah, the sonnet-slave must understand
The mission of his bondage, or the grave
May clasp his bones, or ever he shall save
The perfect word that is the poet's wand!

The sonnet is a crown, whereof the rhymes
Are for Thought's purest gold the jewel-stones;
But shapes and echoes that are never done
Will haunt the workshop, as regret sometimes
Will bring with human yearning to sad thrones
The crash of battles that are never won.

Verlaine

Why do you dig like long-clawed scavengers
To touch the covered corpse of him that fled
The uplands for the fens, and rioted
Like a sick satyr with doom's worshippers?
Come! let the grass grow there; and leave his verse
To tell the story of the life he led.
Let the man go: let the dead flesh be dead,
And let the worms be its biographers.

Song sloughs away the sin to find redress
In art's complete remembrance: nothing clings
For long but laurel to the stricken brow
That felt the Muse's finger; nothing less
Than hell's fulfilment of the end of things
Can blot the star that shines on Paris now.

Sonnet

When we can all so excellently give
The measure of love's wisdom with a blow, —
Why can we not in turn receive it so,
And end this murmur for the life we live?
And when we do so frantically strive
To win strange faith, why do we shun to know
That in love's elemental over-glow
God's wholeness gleams with light superlative?

Oh, brother men, if you have eyes at all,
Look at a branch, a bird, a child, a rose, —
Or anything God ever made that grows, —
Nor let the smallest vision of it slip,
Till you can read, as on Belshazzar's wall,
The glory of eternal partnership!

Supremacy

There is a drear and lonely tract of hell
From all the common gloom removed afar:
A flat, sad land it is, where shadows are,
Whose lorn estate my verse may never tell.
I walked among them and I knew them well:
Men I had slandered on life's little star
For churls and sluggards; and I knew the scar
Upon their brows of woe ineffable.

But as I went majestic on my way,
Into the dark they vanished, one by one,
Till, with a shaft of God's eternal day,
The dream of all my glory was undone, —
And, with a fool's importunate dismay,
I heard the dead men singing in the sun.

The Night Before

Look you, Dominie; look you, and listen!
Look in my face, first; search every line there;
Mark every feature, — chin, lip, and forehead!
Look in my eyes, and tell me the lesson
You read there; measure my nose, and tell me
Where I am wanting! A man's nose, Dominie,
Is often the cast of his inward spirit;
So mark mine well. But why do you smile so?
Pity, or what? Is it written all over,
This face of mine, with a brute's confession?
Nothing but sin there? nothing but hell-scars?
Or is it because there is something better —
A glimmer of good, maybe — or a shadow
Of something that's followed me down from childhood —
Followed me all these years and kept me,
Spite of my slips and sins and follies,
Spite of my last red sin, my murder, —
Just out of hell? Yes? something of that kind?
And you smile for that? You're a good man, Dominie,
The one good man in the world who knows me, —
My one good friend in a world that mocks me,
Here in this hard stone cage. But I leave it
To-morrow. To-morrow! My God! am I crying?
Are these things tears? Tears! What! am I frightened?
I, who swore I should go to the scaffold
With big strong steps, and — No more. I thank you,
But no — I am all right now! No! — listen!
I am here to be hanged; to be hanged to-morrow
At six o'clock, when the sun is rising.
And why am I here? Not a soul can tell you
But this poor shivering thing before you,
This fluttering wreck of the man God made him,
For God knows what wild reason. Hear me,
And learn from my lips the truth of my story.

There's nothing strange in what I shall tell you,
Nothing mysterious, nothing unearthly, —
But damnably human, — and you shall hear it.
Not one of those little black lawyers had guessed it;
The judge, with his big bald head, never knew it;
And the jury (God rest their poor souls!) never dreamed it.
Once there were three in the world who could tell it;
Now there are two. There'll be two to-morrow, —
You, my friend, and — But there's the story: —

When I was a boy the world was heaven.
I never knew then that the men and the women
Who petted and called me a brave big fellow
Were ever less happy than I; but wisdom —
Which comes with the years, you know — soon showed me
The secret of all my glittering childhood,
The broken key to the fairies' castle
That held my life in the fresh, glad season
When I was the king of the earth. Then slowly —
And yet so swiftly! — there came the knowledge
That the marvellous life I had lived was my life;
That the glorious world I had loved was my world;
And that every man, and every woman,
And every child was a different being,
Wrought with a different heat, and fired
With passions born of a single spirit;
That the pleasure I felt was not their pleasure,
Nor my sorrow — a kind of nameless pity
For something, I knew not what — their sorrow.
And thus was I taught my first hard lesson, —
The lesson we suffer the most in learning:
That a happy man is a man forgetful
Of all the torturing ills around him.
When or where I first met the woman
I cherished and made my wife, no matter.
Enough to say that I found her and kept her
Here in my heart with as pure a devotion
As ever Christ felt for his brothers. Forgive me
For naming His name in your patient presence;
But I feel my words, and the truth I utter

Is God's own truth. I loved that woman, —
Not for her face, but for something fairer,
Something diviner, I thought, than beauty:
I loved the spirit — the human something
That seemed to chime with my own condition,
And make soul-music when we were together;
And we were never apart, from the moment
My eyes flashed into her eyes the message
That swept itself in a quivering answer
Back through my strange lost being. My pulses
Leapt with an aching speed; and the measure
Of this great world grew small and smaller,
Till it seemed the sky and the land and the ocean
Closed at last in a mist all golden
Around us two. And we stood for a season
Like gods outflung from chaos, dreaming
That we were the king and the queen of the fire
That reddened the clouds of love that held us
Blind to the new world soon to be ours —
Ours to seize and sway. The passion
Of that great love was a nameless passion,
Bright as the blaze of the sun at noonday,
Wild as the flames of hell; but, mark you,
Never a whit less pure for its fervor.
The baseness in me (for I was human)
Burned like a worm, and perished; and nothing
Was left me then but a soul that mingled
Itself with hers, and swayed and shuddered
In fearful triumph. When I consider
That helpless love and the cursed folly
That wrecked my life for the sake of a woman
Who broke with a laugh the chains of her marriage
(Whatever the word may mean), I wonder
If all the woe was her sin, or whether
The chains themselves were enough to lead her
In love's despite to break them.... Sinners
And saints — I say — are rocked in the cradle,
But never are known till the will within them
Speaks in its own good time. So I foster
Even to-night for the woman who wronged me,

Nothing of hate, nor of love, but a feeling
Of still regret; for the man — But hear me,
And judge for yourself: —

      For a time the seasons
Changed and passed in a sweet succession
That seemed to me like an endless music:
Life was a rolling psalm, and the choirs
Of God were glad for our love. I fancied
All this, and more than I dare to tell you
To-night, — yes, more than I dare to remember;
And then — well, the music stopped. There are moments
In all men's lives when it stops, I fancy, —
Or seems to stop, — till it comes to cheer them
Again with a larger sound. The curtain
Of life just then is lifted a little
To give to their sight new joys — new sorrows —
Or nothing at all, sometimes. I was watching
The slow, sweet scenes of a golden picture,
Flushed and alive with a long delusion
That made the murmur of home, when I shuddered
And felt like a knife that awful silence
That comes when the music goes — forever.
The truth came over my life like a darkness
Over a forest where one man wanders,
Worse than alone. For a time I staggered
And stumbled on with a weak persistence
After the phantom of hope that darted
And dodged like a frightened thing before me,
To quit me at last, and vanish. Nothing
Was left me then but the curse of living
And bearing through all my days the fever
And thirst of a poisoned love. Were I stronger,
Or weaker, perhaps my scorn had saved me,
Given me strength to crush my sorrow
With hate for her and the world that praised her —
To have left her, then and there — to have conquered
That old false life with a new and a wiser, —
Such things are easy in words. You listen,
And frown, I suppose, that I never mention

That beautiful word, FORGIVE! — I forgave her
First of all; and I praised kind Heaven
That I was a brave, clean man to do it;
And then I tried to forget. Forgiveness!
What does it mean when the one forgiven
Shivers and weeps and clings and kisses
The credulous fool that holds her, and tells him
A thousand things of a good man's mercy,
And then slips off with a laugh and plunges
Back to the sin she has quit for a season,
To tell him that hell and the world are better
For her than a prophet's heaven? Believe me,
The love that dies ere its flames are wasted
In search of an alien soul is better,
Better by far than the lonely passion
That burns back into the heart that feeds it.
For I loved her still, and the more she mocked me, —
Fooled with her endless pleading promise
Of future faith, — the more I believed her
The penitent thing she seemed; and the stronger
Her choking arms and her small hot kisses
Bound me and burned my brain to pity,
The more she grew to the heavenly creature
That brightened the life I had lost forever.
The truth was gone somehow for the moment;
The curtain fell for a time; and I fancied
We were again like gods together,
Loving again with the old glad rapture.
But scenes like these, too often repeated,
Failed at last, and her guile was wasted.
I made an end of her shrewd caresses
And told her a few straight words. She took them
Full at their worth — and the farce was over.

. . . . .

At first my dreams of the past upheld me,
But they were a short support: the present
Pushed them away, and I fell. The mission
Of life (whatever it was) was blasted;
My game was lost. And I met the winner
Of that foul deal as a sick slave gathers

63

His painful strength at the sight of his master;
And when he was past I cursed him, fearful
Of that strange chance which makes us mighty
Or mean, or both. I cursed him and hated
The stones he pressed with his heel; I followed
His easy march with a backward envy,
And cursed myself for the beast within me.
But pride is the master of love, and the vision
Of those old days grew faint and fainter:
The counterfeit wife my mercy sheltered
Was nothing now but a woman, — a woman
Out of my way and out of my nature.
My battle with blinded love was over,
My battle with aching pride beginning.
If I was the loser at first, I wonder
If I am the winner now! ... I doubt it.
My life is a losing game; and to-morrow —
To-morrow! — Christ! did I say to-morrow? . . .
Is your brandy good for death? . . . There, — listen: —

When love goes out, and a man is driven
To shun mankind for the scars that make him
A joke for all chattering tongues, he carries
A double burden. The woes I suffered
After that hard betrayal made me
Pity, at first, all breathing creatures
On this bewildered earth. I studied
Their faces and made for myself the story
Of all their scattered lives. Like brothers
And sisters they seemed to me then; and I nourished
A stranger friendship wrought in my fancy
Between those people and me. But somehow,
As time went on, there came queer glances
Out of their eyes, and the shame that stung me
Harassed my pride with a crazed impression
That every face in the surging city
Was turned to me; and I saw sly whispers,
Now and then, as I walked and wearied
My wasted life twice over in bearing
With all my sorrow the sorrows of others, —

Till I found myself their fool. Then I trembled, —
A poor scared thing, — and their prying faces
Told me the ghastly truth: they were laughing
At me and my fate. My God, I could feel it —
That laughter! And then the children caught it;
And I, like a struck dog, crept and listened.
And then when I met the man who had weakened
A woman's love to his own desire,
It seemed to me that all hell were laughing
In fiendish concert! I was their victim —
And his, and hate's. And there was the struggle!
As long as the earth we tread holds something
A tortured heart can love, the meaning
Of life is not wholly blurred; but after
The last loved thing in the world has left us,
We know the triumph of hate. The glory
Of good goes out forever; the beacon
Of sin is the light that leads us downward —
Down to the fiery end. The road runs
Right through hell; and the souls that follow
The cursed ways where its windings lead them
Suffer enough, I say, to merit
All grace that a God can give. — The fashion
Of our belief is to lift all beings
Born for a life that knows no struggle
In sin's tight snares to eternal glory —
All apart from the branded millions
Who carry through life their faces graven
With sure brute scars that tell the story
Of their foul, fated passions. Science
Has yet no salve to smooth or soften
The cradle-scars of a tyrant's visage;
No drug to purge from the vital essence
Of souls the sleeping venom. Virtue
May flower in hell, when its roots are twisted
And wound with the roots of vice; but the stronger
Never is known till there comes that battle
With sin to prove the victor. Perilous
Things are these demons we call our passions:
Slaves are we of their roving fancies,

Fools of their devilish glee. — You think me,
I know, in this maundering way designing
To lighten the load of my guilt and cast it
Half on the shoulders of God. But hear me!
I'm partly a man, — for all my weakness, —
If weakness it were to stand and murder
Before men's eyes the man who had murdered
Me, and driven my burning forehead
With horns for the world to laugh at. Trust me!
And try to believe my words but a portion
Of what God's purpose made me! The coward
Within me cries for this; and I beg you
Now, as I come to the end, to remember
That women and men are on earth to travel
All on a different road. Hereafter
The roads may meet… . I trust in something —
I know not what… .

     Well, this was the way of it: —
Stung with the shame and the secret fury
That comes to the man who has thrown his pittance
Of self at a traitor's feet, I wandered
Weeks and weeks in a baffled frenzy,
Till at last the devil spoke. I heard him,
And laughed at the love that strove to touch me, —
The dead, lost love; and I gripped the demon
Close to my breast, and held him, praising
The fates and the furies that gave me the courage
To follow his wild command. Forgetful
Of all to come when the work was over, —
There came to me then no stony vision
Of these three hundred days, — I cherished
An awful joy in my brain. I pondered
And weighed the thing in my mind, and gloried
In life to think that I was to conquer
Death at his own dark door, — and chuckled
To think of it done so cleanly. One evening
I knew that my time had come. I shuddered
A little, but rather for doubt than terror,
And followed him, — led by the nameless devil

I worshipped and called my brother. The city
Shone like a dream that night; the windows
Flashed with a piercing flame, and the pavements
Pulsed and swayed with a warmth — or something
That seemed so then to my feet — and thrilled me
With a quick, dizzy joy; and the women
And men, like marvellous things of magic,
Floated and laughed and sang by my shoulder,
Sent with a wizard motion. Through it
And over and under it all there sounded
A murmur of life, like bees; and I listened
And laughed again to think of the flower
That grew, blood-red, for me! ... This fellow
Was one of the popular sort who flourish
Unruffled where gods would fall. For a conscience
He carried a snug deceit that made him
The man of the time and the place, whatever
The time or the place might be. Were he sounding,
With a genial craft that cloaked its purpose,
Nigh to itself, the depth of a woman
Fooled with his brainless art, or sending
The midnight home with songs and bottles, —
The cad was there, and his ease forever
Shone with the smooth and slippery polish
That tells the snake. That night he drifted
Into an up-town haunt and ordered —
Whatever it was — with a soft assurance
That made me mad as I stood behind him,
Gripping his death, and waited. Coward,
I think, is the name the world has given
To men like me; but I'll swear I never
Thought of my own disgrace when I shot him —
Yes, in the back, — I know it, I know it
Now; but what if I do? ... As I watched him
Lying there dead in the scattered sawdust,
Wet with a day's blown froth, I noted
That things were still; that the walnut tables,
Where men but a moment before were sitting,
Were gone; that a screen of something around me
Shut them out of my sight. But the gilded

Signs of a hundred beers and whiskeys
Flashed from the walls above, and the mirrors
And glasses behind the bar were lighted
In some strange way, and into my spirit
A thousand shafts of terrible fire
Burned like death, and I fell. The story
Of what came then, you know.

       But tell me,
What does the whole thing mean? What are we, —
Slaves of an awful ignorance? puppets
Pulled by a fiend? or gods, without knowing it?
Do we shut from ourselves our own salvation, —
Or what do we do! I tell you, Dominie,
There are times in the lives of us poor devils
When heaven and hell get mixed. Though conscience
May come like a whisper of Christ to warn us
Away from our sins, it is lost or laughed at, —
And then we fall. And for all who have fallen —
Even for him — I hold no malice,
Nor much compassion: a mightier mercy
Than mine must shrive him. — And I — I am going
Into the light? — or into the darkness?
Why do I sit through these sickening hours,
And hope? Good God! are they hours? — hours?
Yes! I am done with days. And to-morrow —
We two may meet! To-morrow! — To-morrow! …

Walt Whitman

The master-songs are ended, and the man
That sang them is a name. And so is God
A name; and so is love, and life, and death,
And everything. But we, who are too blind
To read what we have written, or what faith
Has written for us, do not understand:
We only blink, and wonder.

Last night it was the song that was the man,
But now it is the man that is the song.
We do not hear him very much to-day:
His piercing and eternal cadence rings
Too pure for us — too powerfully pure,
Too lovingly triumphant, and too large;
But there are some that hear him, and they know
That he shall sing to-morrow for all men,
And that all time shall listen.

The master-songs are ended? Rather say
No songs are ended that are ever sung,
And that no names are dead names. When we write
Men's letters on proud marble or on sand,
We write them there forever.

The Chorus of Old Men in "Aegeus"

Ye gods that have a home beyond the world,
Ye that have eyes for all man's agony,
Ye that have seen this woe that we have seen, —
Look with a just regard,
And with an even grace,
Here on the shattered corpse of a shattered king,
Here on a suffering world where men grow old
And wander like sad shadows till, at last,
Out of the flare of life,
Out of the whirl of years,
Into the mist they go,
Into the mist of death.

O shades of you that loved him long before
The cruel threads of that black sail were spun,
May loyal arms and ancient welcomings
Receive him once again
Who now no longer moves
Here in this flickering dance of changing days,
Where a battle is lost and won for a withered wreath,
And the black master Death is over all,
To chill with his approach,
To level with his touch,
The reigning strength of youth,
The fluttered heart of age.

Woe for the fateful day when Delphi's word was lost —
Woe for the loveless prince of Aethra's line!
Woe for a father's tears and the curse of a king's release —
Woe for the wings of pride and the shafts of doom! —
And thou, the saddest wind
That ever blew from Crete,
Sing the fell tidings back to that thrice unhappy ship! —
Sing to the western flame,

Sing to the dying foam,
A dirge for the sundered years and a dirge for the years to be!

Better his end had been as the end of a cloudless day,
Bright, by the word of Zeus, with a golden star,
Wrought of a golden fame, and flung to the central sky,
To gleam on a stormless tomb for evermore: —
Whether or not there fell
To the touch of an alien hand
The sheen of his purple robe and the shine of his diadem,
Better his end had been
To die as an old man dies, —
But the fates are ever the fates, and a crown is ever a crown.

The Wilderness

Come away! come away! there's a frost along the marshes,
And a frozen wind that skims the shoal where it shakes the dead black
　　water;
There's a moan across the lowland and a wailing through the woodland
Of a dirge that sings to send us back to the arms of those that love us.
There is nothing left but ashes now where the crimson chills of autumn
Put off the summer's languor with a touch that made us glad
For the glory that is gone from us, with a flight we cannot follow,
To the slopes of other valleys and the sounds of other shores.

　　Come away! come away! you can hear them calling, calling,
　　Calling us to come to them, and roam no more.
　　Over there beyond the ridges and the land that lies between us,
　　There's an old song calling us to come!

Come away! come away! — for the scenes we leave behind us
Are barren for the lights of home and a flame that's young forever;
And the lonely trees around us creak the warning of the night-wind,
That love and all the dreams of love are away beyond the mountains.
The songs that call for us to-night, they have called for men before us,
And the winds that blow the message, they have blown ten thousand
　　years;
But this will end our wander-time, for we know the joy that waits us
In the strangeness of home-coming, and a faithful woman's eyes.

　　Come away! come away! there is nothing now to cheer us —
　　Nothing now to comfort us, but love's road home: —
　　Over there beyond the darkness there's a window gleams to greet us,
　　And a warm hearth waits for us within.

Come away! come away! — or the roving-fiend will hold us,
And make us all to dwell with him to the end of human faring:
There are no men yet can leave him when his hands are clutched upon
　　them,

There are none will own his enmity, there are none will call him brother.
So we'll be up and on the way, and the less we brag the better
For the freedom that God gave us and the dread we do not know: —
The frost that skips the willow-leaf will again be back to blight it,
And the doom we cannot fly from is the doom we do not see.

Come away! come away! there are dead men all around us —
Frozen men that mock us with a wild, hard laugh
That shrieks and sinks and whimpers in the shrill November rushes,
And the long fall wind on the lake.

Octaves

I

To get at the eternal strength of things,
And fearlessly to make strong songs of it,
Is, to my mind, the mission of that man
The world would call a poet. He may sing
But roughly, and withal ungraciously;
But if he touch to life the one right chord
Wherein God's music slumbers, and awake
To truth one drowsed ambition, he sings well.

II

We thrill too strangely at the master's touch;
We shrink too sadly from the larger self
Which for its own completeness agitates
And undetermines us; we do not feel —
We dare not feel it yet — the splendid shame
Of uncreated failure; we forget,
The while we groan, that God's accomplishment
Is always and unfailingly at hand.

III

To mortal ears the plainest word may ring
Fantastic and unheard-of, and as false
And out of tune as ever to our own
Did ring the prayers of man-made maniacs;
But if that word be the plain word of Truth,
It leaves an echo that begets itself,
Persistent in itself and of itself,
Regenerate, reiterate, replete.

IV

Tumultuously void of a clean scheme
Whereon to build, whereof to formulate,
The legion life that riots in mankind
Goes ever plunging upward, up and down,
Most like some crazy regiment at arms,
Undisciplined of aught but Ignorance,
And ever led resourcelessly along
To brainless carnage by drunk trumpeters.

V

To me the groaning of world-worshippers
Rings like a lonely music played in hell
By one with art enough to cleave the walls
Of heaven with his cadence, but without
The wisdom or the will to comprehend
The strangeness of his own perversity,
And all without the courage to deny
The profit and the pride of his defeat.

VI

While we are drilled in error, we are lost
Alike to truth and usefulness. We think
We are great warriors now, and we can brag
Like Titans; but the world is growing young,
And we, the fools of time, are growing with it: —
We do not fight to-day, we only die;
We are too proud of death, and too ashamed
Of God, to know enough to be alive.

VII

There is one battle-field whereon we fall
Triumphant and unconquered; but, alas!
We are too fleshly fearful of ourselves
To fight there till our days are whirled and blurred
By sorrow, and the ministering wheels

Of anguish take us eastward, where the clouds
Of human gloom are lost against the gleam
That shines on Thought's impenetrable mail.

VIII

When we shall hear no more the cradle-songs
Of ages — when the timeless hymns of Love
Defeat them and outsound them — we shall know
The rapture of that large release which all
Right science comprehends; and we shall read,
With unoppressed and unoffended eyes,
That record of All-Soul whereon God writes
In everlasting runes the truth of Him.

IX

The guerdon of new childhood is repose: —
Once he has read the primer of right thought,
A man may claim between two smithy strokes
Beatitude enough to realize
God's parallel completeness in the vague
And incommensurable excellence
That equitably uncreates itself
And makes a whirlwind of the Universe.

X

There is no loneliness: — no matter where
We go, nor whence we come, nor what good friends
Forsake us in the seeming, we are all
At one with a complete companionship;
And though forlornly joyless be the ways
We travel, the compensate spirit-gleams
Of Wisdom shaft the darkness here and there,
Like scattered lamps in unfrequented streets.

XI

When one that you and I had all but sworn
To be the purest thing God ever made
Bewilders us until at last it seems
An angel has come back restigmatized, —
Faith wavers, and we wonder what there is
On earth to make us faithful any more,
But never are quite wise enough to know
The wisdom that is in that wonderment.

XII

Where does a dead man go? — The dead man dies;
But the free life that would no longer feed
On fagots of outburned and shattered flesh
Wakes to a thrilled invisible advance,
Unchained (or fettered else) of memory;
And when the dead man goes it seems to me
'T were better for us all to do away
With weeping, and be glad that he is gone.

XIII

Still through the dusk of dead, blank-legended,
And unremunerative years we search
To get where life begins, and still we groan
Because we do not find the living spark
Where no spark ever was; and thus we die,
Still searching, like poor old astronomers
Who totter off to bed and go to sleep,
To dream of untriangulated stars.

XIV

With conscious eyes not yet sincere enough
To pierce the glimmered cloud that fluctuates
Between me and the glorifying light
That screens itself with knowledge, I discern
The searching rays of wisdom that reach through

The mist of shame's infirm credulity,
And infinitely wonder if hard words
Like mine have any message for the dead.

XV

I grant you friendship is a royal thing,
But none shall ever know that royalty
For what it is till he has realized
His best friend in himself. 'T is then, perforce,
That man's unfettered faith indemnifies
Of its own conscious freedom the old shame,
And love's revealed infinitude supplants
Of its own wealth and wisdom the old scorn.

XVI

Though the sick beast infect us, we are fraught
Forever with indissoluble Truth,
Wherein redress reveals itself divine,
Transitional, transcendent. Grief and loss,
Disease and desolation, are the dreams
Of wasted excellence; and every dream
Has in it something of an ageless fact
That flouts deformity and laughs at years.

XVII

We lack the courage to be where we are: —
We love too much to travel on old roads,
To triumph on old fields; we love too much
To consecrate the magic of dead things,
And yieldingly to linger by long walls
Of ruin, where the ruinous moonlight
That sheds a lying glory on old stones
Befriends us with a wizard's enmity.

XVIII

Something as one with eyes that look below
The battle-smoke to glimpse the foeman's charge,
We through the dust of downward years may scan
The onslaught that awaits this idiot world
Where blood pays blood for nothing, and where life
Pays life to madness, till at last the ports
Of gilded helplessness be battered through
By the still crash of salvatory steel.

XIX

To you that sit with Sorrow like chained slaves,
And wonder if the night will ever come,
I would say this: The night will never come,
And sorrow is not always. But my words
Are not enough; your eyes are not enough;
The soul itself must insulate the Real,
Or ever you do cherish in this life —
In this life or in any life — repose.

XX

Like a white wall whereon forever breaks
Unsatisfied the tumult of green seas,
Man's unconjectured godliness rebukes
With its imperial silence the lost waves
Of insufficient grief. This mortal surge
That beats against us now is nothing else
Than plangent ignorance. Truth neither shakes
Nor wavers; but the world shakes, and we shriek.

XXI

Nor jewelled phrase nor mere mellifluous rhyme
Reverberates aright, or ever shall,
One cadence of that infinite plain-song
Which is itself all music. Stronger notes
Than any that have ever touched the world

Must ring to tell it — ring like hammer-blows,
Right-echoed of a chime primordial,
On anvils, in the gleaming of God's forge.

XXII

The prophet of dead words defeats himself:
Whoever would acknowledge and include
The foregleam and the glory of the real,
Must work with something else than pen and ink
And painful preparation: he must work
With unseen implements that have no names,
And he must win withal, to do that work,
Good fortitude, clean wisdom, and strong skill.

XXIII

To curse the chilled insistence of the dawn
Because the free gleam lingers; to defraud
The constant opportunity that lives
Unchallenged in all sorrow; to forget
For this large prodigality of gold
That larger generosity of thought, —
These are the fleshly clogs of human greed,
The fundamental blunders of mankind.

XXIV

Forebodings are the fiends of Recreance;
The master of the moment, the clean seer
Of ages, too securely scans what is,
Ever to be appalled at what is not;
He sees beyond the groaning borough lines
Of Hell, God's highways gleaming, and he knows
That Love's complete communion is the end
Of anguish to the liberated man.

XXV

Here by the windy docks I stand alone,
But yet companioned. There the vessel goes,
And there my friend goes with it; but the wake
That melts and ebbs between that friend and me
Love's earnest is of Life's all-purposeful
And all-triumphant sailing, when the ships
Of Wisdom loose their fretful chains and swing
Forever from the crumbled wharves of Time.

Two Quatrains

I

Unity

As eons of incalculable strife
Are in the vision of one moment caught,
So are the common, concrete things of life
Divinely shadowed on the walls of Thought.

II

Paraphrase

We shriek to live, but no man ever lives
Till he has rid the ghost of human breath;
We dream to die, but no man ever dies
Till he has quit the road that runs to death.

Romance

I

Boys

We were all boys, and three of us were friends;
And we were more than friends, it seemed to me: —
Yes, we were more than brothers then, we three... .
Brothers? . . . But we were boys, and there it ends.

II

James Wetherell

We never half believed the stuff
They told about James Wetherell;
We always liked him well enough,
And always tried to use him well;
But now some things have come to light,
And James has vanished from our view, —
There isn't very much to write,
There isn't very much to do.

The Torrent

I found a torrent falling in a glen
Where the sun's light shone silvered and leaf-split;
The boom, the foam, and the mad flash of it
All made a magic symphony; but when
I thought upon the coming of hard men
To cut those patriarchal trees away,
And turn to gold the silver of that spray,
I shuddered. Yet a gladness now and then
Did wake me to myself till I was glad
In earnest, and was welcoming the time
For screaming saws to sound above the chime
Of idle waters, and for me to know
The jealous visionings that I had had
Were steps to the great place where trees and torrents go.

L'Envoi

Now in a thought, now in a shadowed word,
Now in a voice that thrills eternity,
Ever there comes an onward phrase to me
Of some transcendent music I have heard;
No piteous thing by soft hands dulcimered,
No trumpet crash of blood-sick victory,
But a glad strain of some still symphony
That no proud mortal touch has ever stirred.

There is no music in the world like this,
No character wherewith to set it down,
No kind of instrument to make it sing.
No kind of instrument? Ah, yes, there is!
And after time and place are overthrown,
God's touch will keep its one chord quivering.

The Three Taverns

A Book of Poems

1869-1935

To *Thomas Serteant Perry* and *Lilla Cabot Perry*

The Valley of the Shadow

There were faces to remember in the Valley of the Shadow,
There were faces unregarded, there were faces to forget;
There were fires of grief and fear that are a few forgotten ashes,
There were sparks of recognition that are not forgotten yet.
For at first, with an amazed and overwhelming indignation
At a measureless malfeasance that obscurely willed it thus,
They were lost and unacquainted — till they found themselves in others,
Who had groped as they were groping where dim ways were perilous.

There were lives that were as dark as are the fears and intuitions
Of a child who knows himself and is alone with what he knows;
There were pensioners of dreams and there were debtors of illusions,
All to fail before the triumph of a weed that only grows.
There were thirsting heirs of golden sieves that held not wine or water,
And had no names in traffic or more value there than toys:
There were blighted sons of wonder in the Valley of the Shadow,
Where they suffered and still wondered why their wonder made no noise.

There were slaves who dragged the shackles of a precedent unbroken,
Demonstrating the fulfilment of unalterable schemes,

Which had been, before the cradle, Time's inexorable tenants
Of what were now the dusty ruins of their father's dreams.
There were these, and there were many who had stumbled up to manhood,
Where they saw too late the road they should have taken long ago:
There were thwarted clerks and fiddlers in the Valley of the Shadow,
The commemorative wreckage of what others did not know.

And there were daughters older than the mothers who had borne them,
Being older in their wisdom, which is older than the earth;
And they were going forward only farther into darkness,
Unrelieved as were the blasting obligations of their birth;
And among them, giving always what was not for their possession,
There were maidens, very quiet, with no quiet in their eyes:
There were daughters of the silence in the Valley of the Shadow,
Each an isolated item in the family sacrifice.

There were creepers among catacombs where dull regrets were torches,
Giving light enough to show them what was there upon the shelves —
Where there was more for them to see than pleasure would remember
Of something that had been alive and once had been themselves.
There were some who stirred the ruins with a solid imprecation,
While as many fled repentance for the promise of despair:
There were drinkers of wrong waters in the Valley of the Shadow,
And all the sparkling ways were dust that once had led them there.

There were some who knew the steps of Age incredibly beside them,
And his fingers upon shoulders that had never felt the wheel;
And their last of empty trophies was a gilded cup of nothing,
Which a contemplating vagabond would not have come to steal.
Long and often had they figured for a larger valuation,
But the size of their addition was the balance of a doubt:
There were gentlemen of leisure in the Valley of the Shadow,
Not allured by retrospection, disenchanted, and played out.

And among the dark endurances of unavowed reprisals
There were silent eyes of envy that saw little but saw well;
And over beauty's aftermath of hazardous ambitions
There were tears for what had vanished as they vanished where they fell.
Not assured of what was theirs, and always hungry for the nameless,
There were some whose only passion was for Time who made them cold:

There were numerous fair women in the Valley of the Shadow,
Dreaming rather less of heaven than of hell when they were old.

Now and then, as if to scorn the common touch of common sorrow,
There were some who gave a few the distant pity of a smile;
And another cloaked a soul as with an ash of human embers,
Having covered thus a treasure that would last him for a while.
There were many by the presence of the many disaffected,
Whose exemption was included in the weight that others bore:
There were seekers after darkness in the Valley of the Shadow,
And they alone were there to find what they were looking for.

So they were, and so they are; and as they came are coming others,
And among them are the fearless and the meek and the unborn;
And a question that has held us heretofore without an answer
May abide without an answer until all have ceased to mourn.
For the children of the dark are more to name than are the wretched,
Or the broken, or the weary, or the baffled, or the shamed:
There are builders of new mansions in the Valley of the Shadow,
And among them are the dying and the blinded and the maimed.

The Wandering Jew

I saw by looking in his eyes
That they remembered everything;
And this was how I came to know
That he was here, still wandering.
For though the figure and the scene
Were never to be reconciled,
I knew the man as I had known
His image when I was a child.

With evidence at every turn,
I should have held it safe to guess
That all the newness of New York
Had nothing new in loneliness;
Yet here was one who might be Noah,
Or Nathan, or Abimelech,
Or Lamech, out of ages lost, —
Or, more than all, Melchizedek.

Assured that he was none of these,
I gave them back their names again,
To scan once more those endless eyes
Where all my questions ended then.
I found in them what they revealed
That I shall not live to forget,
And wondered if they found in mine
Compassion that I might regret.

Pity, I learned, was not the least
Of time's offending benefits
That had now for so long impugned
The conservation of his wits:
Rather it was that I should yield,
Alone, the fealty that presents
The tribute of a tempered ear

To an untempered eloquence.

Before I pondered long enough
On whence he came and who he was,
I trembled at his ringing wealth
Of manifold anathemas;
I wondered, while he seared the world,
What new defection ailed the race,
And if it mattered how remote
Our fathers were from such a place.

Before there was an hour for me
To contemplate with less concern
The crumbling realm awaiting us
Than his that was beyond return,
A dawning on the dust of years
Had shaped with an elusive light
Mirages of remembered scenes
That were no longer for the sight.

For now the gloom that hid the man
Became a daylight on his wrath,
And one wherein my fancy viewed
New lions ramping in his path.
The old were dead and had no fangs,
Wherefore he loved them — seeing not
They were the same that in their time
Had eaten everything they caught.

The world around him was a gift
Of anguish to his eyes and ears,
And one that he had long reviled
As fit for devils, not for seers.
Where, then, was there a place for him
That on this other side of death
Saw nothing good, as he had seen
No good come out of Nazareth?

Yet here there was a reticence,
And I believe his only one,

That hushed him as if he beheld
A Presence that would not be gone.
In such a silence he confessed
How much there was to be denied;
And he would look at me and live,
As others might have looked and died.

As if at last he knew again
That he had always known, his eyes
Were like to those of one who gazed
On those of One who never dies.
For such a moment he revealed
What life has in it to be lost;
And I could ask if what I saw,
Before me there, was man or ghost.

He may have died so many times
That all there was of him to see
Was pride, that kept itself alive
As too rebellious to be free;
He may have told, when more than once
Humility seemed imminent,
How many a lonely time in vain
The Second Coming came and went.

Whether he still defies or not
The failure of an angry task
That relegates him out of time
To chaos, I can only ask.
But as I knew him, so he was;
And somewhere among men to-day
Those old, unyielding eyes may flash,
And flinch — and look the other way.

Neighbors

As often as we thought of her,
 We thought of a gray life
That made a quaint economist
 Of a wolf-haunted wife;
We made the best of all she bore

91

That was not ours to bear,
And honored her for wearing things
That were not things to wear.

There was a distance in her look
  That made us look again;
And if she smiled, we might believe
  That we had looked in vain.
Rarely she came inside our doors,
  And had not long to stay;
And when she left, it seemed somehow
  That she was far away.

At last, when we had all forgot
  That all is here to change,
A shadow on the commonplace
  Was for a moment strange.
Yet there was nothing for surprise,
  Nor much that need be told:
Love, with his gift of pain, had given
  More than one heart could hold.
The Mill

The miller's wife had waited long,
  The tea was cold, the fire was dead;
And there might yet be nothing wrong
  In how he went and what he said:
"There are no millers any more,"
  Was all that she had heard him say;
And he had lingered at the door
  So long that it seemed yesterday.

Sick with a fear that had no form
  She knew that she was there at last;
And in the mill there was a warm
  And mealy fragrance of the past.
What else there was would only seem
  To say again what he had meant;
And what was hanging from a beam
  Would not have heeded where she went.

And if she thought it followed her,
 She may have reasoned in the dark
That one way of the few there were
 Would hide her and would leave no mark:
Black water, smooth above the weir
 Like starry velvet in the night,
Though ruffled once, would soon appear
 The same as ever to the sight.
The Dark Hills

Dark hills at evening in the west,
Where sunset hovers like a sound
Of golden horns that sang to rest
Old bones of warriors under ground,
Far now from all the bannered ways
Where flash the legions of the sun,
You fade — as if the last of days
Were fading, and all wars were done.

The Three Taverns

When the brethren heard of us, they came to meet us as far as
Appii Forum, and The Three Taverns.

(Acts 28:15)

Herodion, Apelles, Amplias,
And Andronicus? Is it you I see —
At last? And is it you now that are gazing
As if in doubt of me? Was I not saying
That I should come to Rome? I did say that;
And I said furthermore that I should go
On westward, where the gateway of the world
Lets in the central sea. I did say that,
But I say only, now, that I am Paul —
A prisoner of the Law, and of the Lord
A voice made free. If there be time enough
To live, I may have more to tell you then
Of western matters. I go now to Rome,
Where Caesar waits for me, and I shall wait,
And Caesar knows how long. In Caesarea
There was a legend of Agrippa saying
In a light way to Festus, having heard
My deposition, that I might be free,
Had I stayed free of Caesar; but the word
Of God would have it as you see it is —
And here I am. The cup that I shall drink
Is mine to drink — the moment or the place
Not mine to say. If it be now in Rome,
Be it now in Rome; and if your faith exceed
The shadow cast of hope, say not of me
Too surely or too soon that years and shipwreck,
And all the many deserts I have crossed
That are not named or regioned, have undone

Beyond the brevities of our mortal healing
The part of me that is the least of me.
You see an older man than he who fell
Prone to the earth when he was nigh Damascus,
Where the great light came down; yet I am he
That fell, and he that saw, and he that heard.
And I am here, at last; and if at last
I give myself to make another crumb
For this pernicious feast of time and men —
Well, I have seen too much of time and men
To fear the ravening or the wrath of either.

Yes, it is Paul you see — the Saul of Tarsus
That was a fiery Jew, and had men slain
For saying Something was beyond the Law,
And in ourselves. I fed my suffering soul
Upon the Law till I went famishing,
Not knowing that I starved. How should I know,
More then than any, that the food I had —
What else it may have been — was not for me?
My fathers and their fathers and their fathers
Had found it good, and said there was no other,
And I was of the line. When Stephen fell,
Among the stones that crushed his life away,
There was no place alive that I could see
For such a man. Why should a man be given
To live beyond the Law? So I said then,
As men say now to me. How then do I
Persist in living? Is that what you ask?
If so, let my appearance be for you
No living answer; for Time writes of death
On men before they die, and what you see
Is not the man. The man that you see not —
The man within the man — is most alive;
Though hatred would have ended, long ago,
The bane of his activities. I have lived,
Because the faith within me that is life
Endures to live, and shall, till soon or late,
Death, like a friend unseen, shall say to me
My toil is over and my work begun.

How often, and how many a time again,
Have I said I should be with you in Rome!
He who is always coming never comes,
Or comes too late, you may have told yourselves;
And I may tell you now that after me,
Whether I stay for little or for long,
The wolves are coming. Have an eye for them,
And a more careful ear for their confusion
Than you need have much longer for the sound
Of what I tell you — should I live to say
More than I say to Caesar. What I know
Is down for you to read in what is written;
And if I cloud a little with my own
Mortality the gleam that is immortal,
I do it only because I am I —
Being on earth and of it, in so far
As time flays yet the remnant. This you know;
And if I sting men, as I do sometimes,
With a sharp word that hurts, it is because
Man's habit is to feel before he sees;
And I am of a race that feels. Moreover,
The world is here for what is not yet here
For more than are a few; and even in Rome,
Where men are so enamored of the Cross
That fame has echoed, and increasingly,
The music of your love and of your faith
To foreign ears that are as far away
As Antioch and Haran, yet I wonder
How much of love you know, and if your faith
Be the shut fruit of words. If so, remember
Words are but shells unfilled. Jews have at least
A Law to make them sorry they were born
If they go long without it; and these Gentiles,
For the first time in shrieking history,
Have love and law together, if so they will,
For their defense and their immunity
In these last days. Rome, if I know the name,
Will have anon a crown of thorns and fire
Made ready for the wreathing of new masters,

Of whom we are appointed, you and I, —
And you are still to be when I am gone,
Should I go presently. Let the word fall,
Meanwhile, upon the dragon-ridden field
Of circumstance, either to live or die;
Concerning which there is a parable,
Made easy for the comfort and attention
Of those who preach, fearing they preach in vain.
You are to plant, and then to plant again
Where you have gathered, gathering as you go;
For you are in the fields that are eternal,
And you have not the burden of the Lord
Upon your mortal shoulders. What you have
Is a light yoke, made lighter by the wearing,
Till it shall have the wonder and the weight
Of a clear jewel, shining with a light
Wherein the sun and all the fiery stars
May soon be fading. When Gamaliel said
That if they be of men these things are nothing,
But if they be of God they are for none
To overthrow, he spoke as a good Jew,
And one who stayed a Jew; and he said all.
And you know, by the temper of your faith,
How far the fire is in you that I felt
Before I knew Damascus. A word here,
Or there, or not there, or not anywhere,
Is not the Word that lives and is the life;
And you, therefore, need weary not yourselves
With jealous aches of others. If the world
Were not a world of aches and innovations,
Attainment would have no more joy of it.
There will be creeds and schisms, creeds in creeds,
And schisms in schisms; myriads will be done
To death because a farthing has two sides,
And is at last a farthing. Telling you this,
I, who bid men to live, appeal to Caesar.
Once I had said the ways of God were dark,
Meaning by that the dark ways of the Law.
Such is the glory of our tribulations;
For the Law kills the flesh that kills the Law,

And we are then alive. We have eyes then;
And we have then the Cross between two worlds —
To guide us, or to blind us for a time,
Till we have eyes indeed. The fire that smites
A few on highways, changing all at once,
Is not for all. The power that holds the world
Away from God that holds himself away —
Farther away than all your works and words
Are like to fly without the wings of faith —
Was not, nor ever shall be, a small hazard
Enlivening the ways of easy leisure
Or the cold road of knowledge. When our eyes
Have wisdom, we see more than we remember;
And the old world of our captivities
May then become a smitten glimpse of ruin,
Like one where vanished hewers have had their day
Of wrath on Lebanon. Before we see,
Meanwhile, we suffer; and I come to you,
At last, through many storms and through much night.

Yet whatsoever I have undergone,
My keepers in this instance are not hard.
But for the chance of an ingratitude,
I might indeed be curious of their mercy,
And fearful of their leisure while I wait,
A few leagues out of Rome. Men go to Rome,
Not always to return — but not that now.
Meanwhile, I seem to think you look at me
With eyes that are at last more credulous
Of my identity. You remark in me
No sort of leaping giant, though some words
Of mine to you from Corinth may have leapt
A little through your eyes into your soul.
I trust they were alive, and are alive
Today; for there be none that shall indite
So much of nothing as the man of words
Who writes in the Lord's name for his name's sake
And has not in his blood the fire of time
To warm eternity. Let such a man —
If once the light is in him and endures —

Content himself to be the general man,
Set free to sift the decencies and thereby
To learn, except he be one set aside
For sorrow, more of pleasure than of pain;
Though if his light be not the light indeed,
But a brief shine that never really was,
And fails, leaving him worse than where he was,
Then shall he be of all men destitute.
And here were not an issue for much ink,
Or much offending faction among scribes.

The Kingdom is within us, we are told;
And when I say to you that we possess it
In such a measure as faith makes it ours,
I say it with a sinner's privilege
Of having seen and heard, and seen again,
After a darkness; and if I affirm
To the last hour that faith affords alone
The Kingdom entrance and an entertainment,
I do not see myself as one who says
To man that he shall sit with folded hands
Against the Coming. If I be anything,
I move a driven agent among my kind,
Establishing by the faith of Abraham,
And by the grace of their necessities,
The clamoring word that is the word of life
Nearer than heretofore to the solution
Of their tomb-serving doubts. If I have loosed
A shaft of language that has flown sometimes
A little higher than the hearts and heads
Of nature's minions, it will yet be heard,
Like a new song that waits for distant ears.
I cannot be the man that I am not;
And while I own that earth is my affliction,
I am a man of earth, who says not all
To all alike. That were impossible,
Even as it were so that He should plant
A larger garden first. But you today
Are for the larger sowing; and your seed,
A little mixed, will have, as He foresaw,

The foreign harvest of a wider growth,
And one without an end. Many there are,
And are to be, that shall partake of it,
Though none may share it with an understanding
That is not his alone. We are all alone;
And yet we are all parcelled of one order —
Jew, Gentile, or barbarian in the dark
Of wildernesses that are not so much
As names yet in a book. And there are many,
Finding at last that words are not the Word,
And finding only that, will flourish aloft,
Like heads of captured Pharisees on pikes,
Our contradictions and discrepancies;
And there are many more will hang themselves
Upon the letter, seeing not in the Word
The friend of all who fail, and in their faith
A sword of excellence to cut them down.

As long as there are glasses that are dark —
And there are many — we see darkly through them;
All which have I conceded and set down
In words that have no shadow. What is dark
Is dark, and we may not say otherwise;
Yet what may be as dark as a lost fire
For one of us, may still be for another
A coming gleam across the gulf of ages,
And a way home from shipwreck to the shore;
And so, through pangs and ills and desperations,
There may be light for all. There shall be light.
As much as that, you know. You cannot say
This woman or that man will be the next
On whom it falls; you are not here for that.
Your ministration is to be for others
The firing of a rush that may for them
Be soon the fire itself. The few at first
Are fighting for the multitude at last;
Therefore remember what Gamaliel said
Before you, when the sick were lying down
In streets all night for Peter's passing shadow.
Fight, and say what you feel; say more than words.

Give men to know that even their days of earth
To come are more than ages that are gone.
Say what you feel, while you have time to say it.
Eternity will answer for itself,
Without your intercession; yet the way
For many is a long one, and as dark,
Meanwhile, as dreams of hell. See not your toil
Too much, and if I be away from you,
Think of me as a brother to yourselves,
Of many blemishes. Beware of stoics,
And give your left hand to grammarians;
And when you seem, as many a time you may,
To have no other friend than hope, remember
That you are not the first, or yet the last.

The best of life, until we see beyond
The shadows of ourselves (and they are less
Than even the blindest of indignant eyes
Would have them) is in what we do not know.
Make, then, for all your fears a place to sleep
With all your faded sins; nor think yourselves
Egregious and alone for your defects
Of youth and yesterday. I was young once;
And there's a question if you played the fool
With a more fervid and inherent zeal
Than I have in my story to remember,
Or gave your necks to folly's conquering foot,
Or flung yourselves with an unstudied aim,
Less frequently than I. Never mind that.
Man's little house of days will hold enough,
Sometimes, to make him wish it were not his,
But it will not hold all. Things that are dead
Are best without it, and they own their death
By virtue of their dying. Let them go, —
But think you not the world is ashes yet,
And you have all the fire. The world is here
Today, and it may not be gone tomorrow;
For there are millions, and there may be more,
To make in turn a various estimation
Of its old ills and ashes, and the traps

Of its apparent wrath. Many with ears
That hear not yet, shall have ears given to them,
And then they shall hear strangely. Many with eyes
That are incredulous of the Mystery
Shall yet be driven to feel, and then to read
Where language has an end and is a veil,
Not woven of our words. Many that hate
Their kind are soon to know that without love
Their faith is but the perjured name of nothing.
I that have done some hating in my time
See now no time for hate; I that have left,
Fading behind me like familiar lights
That are to shine no more for my returning,
Home, friends, and honors, — I that have lost all else
For wisdom, and the wealth of it, say now
To you that out of wisdom has come love,
That measures and is of itself the measure
Of works and hope and faith. Your longest hours
Are not so long that you may torture them
And harass not yourselves; and the last days
Are on the way that you prepare for them,
And was prepared for you, here in a world
Where you have sinned and suffered, striven and seen.
If you be not so hot for counting them
Before they come that you consume yourselves,
Peace may attend you all in these last days —
And me, as well as you. Yes, even in Rome.
Well, I have talked and rested, though I fear
My rest has not been yours; in which event,
Forgive one who is only seven leagues
From Caesar. When I told you I should come,
I did not see myself the criminal
You contemplate, for seeing beyond the Law
That which the Law saw not. But this, indeed,
Was good of you, and I shall not forget;
No, I shall not forget you came so far
To meet a man so dangerous. Well, farewell.
They come to tell me I am going now —
With them. I hope that we shall meet again,
But none may say what he shall find in Rome.

Demos I

All you that are enamored of my name
 And least intent on what most I require,
 Beware; for my design and your desire,
Deplorably, are not as yet the same.
Beware, I say, the failure and the shame
 Of losing that for which you now aspire
 So blindly, and of hazarding entire
The gift that I was bringing when I came.

Give as I will, I cannot give you sight
 Whereby to see that with you there are some
 To lead you, and be led. But they are dumb
Before the wrangling and the shrill delight
 Of your deliverance that has not come,
And shall not, if I fail you — as I might.

Demos II

So little have you seen of what awaits
 Your fevered glimpse of a democracy
 Confused and foiled with an equality
Not equal to the envy it creates,
That you see not how near you are the gates
 Of an old king who listens fearfully
 To you that are outside and are to be
The noisy lords of imminent estates.

Rather be then your prayer that you shall have
 Your kingdom undishonored. Having all,
 See not the great among you for the small,
But hear their silence; for the few shall save
 The many, or the many are to fall —
Still to be wrangling in a noisy grave.

The Flying Dutchman

Unyielding in the pride of his defiance,
 Afloat with none to serve or to command,
Lord of himself at last, and all by Science,
 He seeks the Vanished Land.

Alone, by the one light of his one thought,
 He steers to find the shore from which we came, —
Fearless of in what coil he may be caught
 On seas that have no name.

Into the night he sails; and after night
 There is a dawning, though there be no sun;
Wherefore, with nothing but himself in sight,
 Unsighted, he sails on.

At last there is a lifting of the cloud
 Between the flood before him and the sky;
And then — though he may curse the Power aloud
 That has no power to die —

He steers himself away from what is haunted
 By the old ghost of what has been before, —
Abandoning, as always, and undaunted,
 One fog-walled island more.

Tact

Observant of the way she told
 So much of what was true,
No vanity could long withhold
 Regard that was her due:
She spared him the familiar guile,
 So easily achieved,
That only made a man to smile
 And left him undeceived.

Aware that all imagining
 Of more than what she meant
Would urge an end of everything,
 He stayed; and when he went,
They parted with a merry word
 That was to him as light
As any that was ever heard
 Upon a starry night.

She smiled a little, knowing well
 That he would not remark
The ruins of a day that fell
 Around her in the dark:
He saw no ruins anywhere,
 Nor fancied there were scars
On anyone who lingered there,
 Alone below the stars.

On the Way

(Philadelphia, 1794)

Note. — The following imaginary dialogue between Alexander Hamilton and Aaron Burr, which is not based upon any specific incident in American history, may be supposed to have occurred a few months previous to Hamilton's retirement from Washington's Cabinet in 1795 and a few years before the political ingenuities of Burr—who has been characterized, without much exaggeration, as the inventor of American politics — began to be conspicuously formidable to the Federalists. These activities on the part of Burr resulted, as the reader will remember, in the Burr-Jefferson tie for the Presidency in 1800, and finally in the Burr-Hamilton duel at Weehawken in 1804.

BURR

Hamilton, if he rides you down, remember
That I was here to speak, and so to save
Your fabric from catastrophe. That's good;
For I perceive that you observe him also.
A President, a-riding of his horse,
May dust a General and be forgiven;
But why be dusted — when we're all alike,
All equal, and all happy. Here he comes —
And there he goes. And we, by your new parent,
Would seem to be two kings here by the wayside,
With our two hats off to his Excellency.
Why not his Majesty, and done with it?
Forgive me if I shook your meditation,
But you that weld our credit should have eyes
To see what's coming. Bury me first if -I- do.

HAMILTON

There's always in some pocket of your brain
A care for me; wherefore my gratitude
For your attention is commensurate
With your concern. Yes, Burr, we are two kings;
We are as royal as two ditch-diggers;
But owe me not your sceptre. These are the days
When first a few seem all; but if we live,
We may again be seen to be the few
That we have always been. These are the days
When men forget the stars, and are forgotten.

BURR

But why forget them? They're the same that winked
Upon the world when Alcibiades
Cut off his dog's tail to induce distinction.
There are dogs yet, and Alcibiades
Is not forgotten.

HAMILTON

  Yes, there are dogs enough,
God knows; and I can hear them in my dreams.

BURR

Never a doubt. But what you hear the most
Is your new music, something out of tune
With your intention. How in the name of Cain,
I seem to hear you ask, are men to dance,
When all men are musicians. Tell me that,
I hear you saying, and I'll tell you the name
Of Samson's mother. But why shroud yourself
Before the coffin comes? For all you know,
The tree that is to fall for your last house
Is now a sapling. You may have to wait

So long as to be sorry; though I doubt it,
For you are not at home in your new Eden
Where chilly whispers of a likely frost
Accumulate already in the air.
I think a touch of ermine, Hamilton,
Would be for you in your autumnal mood
A pleasant sort of warmth along the shoulders.

HAMILTON

If so it is you think, you may as well
Give over thinking. We are done with ermine.
What I fear most is not the multitude,
But those who are to loop it with a string
That has one end in France and one end here.
I'm not so fortified with observation
That I could swear that more than half a score
Among us who see lightning see that ruin
Is not the work of thunder. Since the world
Was ordered, there was never a long pause
For caution between doing and undoing.

BURR

Go on, sir; my attention is a trap
Set for the catching of all compliments
To Monticello, and all else abroad
That has a name or an identity.

HAMILTON

I leave to you the names — there are too many;
Yet one there is to sift and hold apart,
As now I see. There comes at last a glimmer
That is not always clouded, or too late.
But I was near and young, and had the reins
To play with while he manned a team so raw
That only God knows where the end had been
Of all that riding without Washington.
There was a nation in the man who passed us,

If there was not a world. I may have driven
Since then some restive horses, and alone,
And through a splashing of abundant mud;
But he who made the dust that sets you on
To coughing, made the road. Now it seems dry,
And in a measure safe.

BURR

      Here's a new tune
From Hamilton. Has your caution all at once,
And over night, grown till it wrecks the cradle?
I have forgotten what my father said
When I was born, but there's a rustling of it
Among my memories, and it makes a noise
About as loud as all that I have held
And fondled heretofore of your same caution.
But that's affairs, not feelings. If our friends
Guessed half we say of them, our enemies
Would itch in our friends' jackets. Howsoever,
The world is of a sudden on its head,
And all are spilled — unless you cling alone
With Washington. Ask Adams about that.

HAMILTON

We'll not ask Adams about anything.
We fish for lizards when we choose to ask
For what we know already is not coming,
And we must eat the answer. Where's the use
Of asking when this man says everything,
With all his tongues of silence?

BURR

      I dare say.
I dare say, but I won't. One of those tongues
I'll borrow for the nonce. He'll never miss it.
We mean his Western Majesty, King George.

HAMILTON

I mean the man who rode by on his horse.
I'll beg of you the meed of your indulgence
If I should say this planet may have done
A deal of weary whirling when at last,
If ever, Time shall aggregate again
A majesty like his that has no name.

BURR

Then you concede his Majesty? That's good,
And what of yours? Here are two majesties.
Favor the Left a little, Hamilton,
Or you'll be floundering in the ditch that waits
For riders who forget where they are riding.
If we and France, as you anticipate,
Must eat each other, what Caesar, if not yourself,
Do you see for the master of the feast?
There may be a place waiting on your head
For laurel thick as Nero's. You don't know.
I have not crossed your glory, though I might
If I saw thrones at auction.

HAMILTON

      Yes, you might.
If war is on the way, I shall be — here;
And I've no vision of your distant heels.

BURR

I see that I shall take an inference
To bed with me to-night to keep me warm.
I thank you, Hamilton, and I approve
Your fealty to the aggregated greatness
Of him you lean on while he leans on you.

HAMILTON

This easy phrasing is a game of yours
That you may win to lose. I beg your pardon,
But you that have the sight will not employ
The will to see with it. If you did so,
There might be fewer ditches dug for others
In your perspective; and there might be fewer
Contemporary motes of prejudice
Between you and the man who made the dust.
Call him a genius or a gentleman,
A prophet or a builder, or what not,
But hold your disposition off the balance,
And weigh him in the light. Once (I believe
I tell you nothing new to your surmise,
Or to the tongues of towns and villages)
I nourished with an adolescent fancy —
Surely forgivable to you, my friend —
An innocent and amiable conviction
That I was, by the grace of honest fortune,
A savior at his elbow through the war,
Where I might have observed, more than I did,
Patience and wholesome passion. I was there,
And for such honor I gave nothing worse
Than some advice at which he may have smiled.
I must have given a modicum besides,
Or the rough interval between those days
And these would never have made for me my friends,
Or enemies. I should be something somewhere —
I say not what — but I should not be here
If he had not been there. Possibly, too,
You might not — or that Quaker with his cane.

BURR

Possibly, too, I should. When the Almighty
Rides a white horse, I fancy we shall know it.

HAMILTON

It was a man, Burr, that was in my mind;
No god, or ghost, or demon — only a man:
A man whose occupation is the need
Of those who would not feel it if it bit them;
And one who shapes an age while he endures
The pin pricks of inferiorities;
A cautious man, because he is but one;
A lonely man, because he is a thousand.
No marvel you are slow to find in him
The genius that is one spark or is nothing:
His genius is a flame that he must hold
So far above the common heads of men
That they may view him only through the mist
Of their defect, and wonder what he is.
It seems to me the mystery that is in him
That makes him only more to me a man
Than any other I have ever known.

BURR

I grant you that his worship is a man.
I'm not so much at home with mysteries,
May be, as you — so leave him with his fire:
God knows that I shall never put it out.
He has not made a cripple of himself
In his pursuit of me, though I have heard
His condescension honors me with parts.
Parts make a whole, if we've enough of them;
And once I figured a sufficiency
To be at least an atom in the annals
Of your republic. But I must have erred.

HAMILTON

You smile as if your spirit lived at ease
With error. I should not have named it so,
Failing assent from you; nor, if I did,
Should I be so complacent in my skill

To comb the tangled language of the people
As to be sure of anything in these days.
Put that much in account with modesty.

BURR

What in the name of Ahab, Hamilton,
Have you, in the last region of your dreaming,
To do with "people"? You may be the devil
In your dead-reckoning of what reefs and shoals
Are waiting on the progress of our ship
Unless you steer it, but you'll find it irksome
Alone there in the stern; and some warm day
There'll be an inland music in the rigging,
And afterwards on deck. I'm not affined
Or favored overmuch at Monticello,
But there's a mighty swarming of new bees
About the premises, and all have wings.
If you hear something buzzing before long,
Be thoughtful how you strike, remembering also
There was a fellow Naboth had a vineyard,
And Ahab cut his hair off and went softly.

HAMILTON

I don't remember that he cut his hair off.

BURR

Somehow I rather fancy that he did.
If so, it's in the Book; and if not so,
He did the rest, and did it handsomely.

HAMILTON

Commend yourself to Ahab and his ways
If they inveigle you to emulation;
But where, if I may ask it, are you tending
With your invidious wielding of the Scriptures?

You call to mind an eminent archangel
Who fell to make him famous. Would you fall
So far as he, to be so far remembered?

BURR

Before I fall or rise, or am an angel,
I shall acquaint myself a little further
With our new land's new language, which is not —
Peace to your dreams — an idiom to your liking.
I'm wondering if a man may always know
How old a man may be at thirty-seven;
I wonder likewise if a prettier time
Could be decreed for a good man to vanish
Than about now for you, before you fade,
And even your friends are seeing that you have had
Your cup too full for longer mortal triumph.
Well, you have had enough, and had it young;
And the old wine is nearer to the lees
Than you are to the work that you are doing.

HAMILTON

When does this philological excursion
Into new lands and languages begin?

BURR

Anon — that is, already. Only Fortune
Gave me this afternoon the benefaction
Of your blue back, which I for love pursued,
And in pursuing may have saved your life —
Also the world a pounding piece of news:
Hamilton bites the dust of Washington,
Or rather of his horse. For you alone,
Or for your fame, I'd wish it might have been so.

HAMILTON

Not every man among us has a friend
So jealous for the other's fame. How long
Are you to diagnose the doubtful case
Of Demos — and what for? Have you a sword
For some new Damocles? If it's for me,
I have lost all official appetite,
And shall have faded, after January,
Into the law. I'm going to New York.

BURR

No matter where you are, one of these days
I shall come back to you and tell you something.
This Demos, I have heard, has in his wrist
A pulse that no two doctors have as yet
Counted and found the same, and in his mouth
A tongue that has the like alacrity
For saying or not for saying what most it is
That pullulates in his ignoble mind.
One of these days I shall appear again,
To tell you more of him and his opinions;
I shall not be so long out of your sight,
Or take myself so far, that I may not,
Like Alcibiades, come back again.
He went away to Phrygia, and fared ill.

HAMILTON

There's an example in Themistocles:
He went away to Persia, and fared well.

BURR

So? Must I go so far? And if so, why so?
I had not planned it so. Is this the road
I take? If so, farewell.

HAMILTON

Quite so. Farewell.

John Brown

Though for your sake I would not have you now
So near to me tonight as now you are,
God knows how much a stranger to my heart
Was any cold word that I may have written;
And you, poor woman that I made my wife,
You have had more of loneliness, I fear,
Than I — though I have been the most alone,
Even when the most attended. So it was
God set the mark of his inscrutable
Necessity on one that was to grope,
And serve, and suffer, and withal be glad
For what was his, and is, and is to be,
When his old bones, that are a burden now,
Are saying what the man who carried them
Had not the power to say. Bones in a grave,
Cover them as they will with choking earth,
May shout the truth to men who put them there,
More than all orators. And so, my dear,
Since you have cheated wisdom for the sake
Of sorrow, let your sorrow be for you,
This last of nights before the last of days,
The lying ghost of what there is of me
That is the most alive. There is no death
For me in what they do. Their death it is
They should heed most when the sun comes again
To make them solemn. There are some I know
Whose eyes will hardly see their occupation,
For tears in them — and all for one old man;
For some of them will pity this old man,
Who took upon himself the work of God
Because he pitied millions. That will be
For them, I fancy, their compassionate
Best way of saying what is best in them
To say; for they can say no more than that,

And they can do no more than what the dawn
Of one more day shall give them light enough
To do. But there are many days to be,
And there are many men to give their blood,
As I gave mine for them. May they come soon!

May they come soon, I say. And when they come,
May all that I have said unheard be heard,
Proving at last, or maybe not — no matter —
What sort of madness was the part of me
That made me strike, whether I found the mark
Or missed it. Meanwhile, I've a strange content,
A patience, and a vast indifference
To what men say of me and what men fear
To say. There was a work to be begun,
And when the Voice, that I have heard so long,
Announced as in a thousand silences
An end of preparation, I began
The coming work of death which is to be,
That life may be. There is no other way
Than the old way of war for a new land
That will not know itself and is tonight
A stranger to itself, and to the world
A more prodigious upstart among states
Than I was among men, and so shall be
Till they are told and told, and told again;
For men are children, waiting to be told,
And most of them are children all their lives.
The good God in his wisdom had them so,
That now and then a madman or a seer
May shake them out of their complacency
And shame them into deeds. The major file
See only what their fathers may have seen,
Or may have said they saw when they saw nothing.
I do not say it matters what they saw.
Now and again to some lone soul or other
God speaks, and there is hanging to be done, —
As once there was a burning of our bodies
Alive, albeit our souls were sorry fuel.
But now the fires are few, and we are poised

Accordingly, for the state's benefit,
A few still minutes between heaven and earth.
The purpose is, when they have seen enough
Of what it is that they are not to see,
To pluck me as an unripe fruit of treason,
And then to fling me back to the same earth
Of which they are, as I suppose, the flower —
Not given to know the riper fruit that waits
For a more comprehensive harvesting.

Yes, may they come, and soon. Again I say,
May they come soon! — before too many of them
Shall be the bloody cost of our defection.
When hell waits on the dawn of a new state,
Better it were that hell should not wait long, —
Or so it is I see it who should see
As far or farther into time tonight
Than they who talk and tremble for me now,
Or wish me to those everlasting fires
That are for me no fear. Too many fires
Have sought me out and seared me to the bone —
Thereby, for all I know, to temper me
For what was mine to do. If I did ill
What I did well, let men say I was mad;
Or let my name for ever be a question
That will not sleep in history. What men say
I was will cool no cannon, dull no sword,
Invalidate no truth. Meanwhile, I was;
And the long train is lighted that shall burn,
Though floods of wrath may drench it, and hot feet
May stamp it for a slight time into smoke
That shall blaze up again with growing speed,
Until at last a fiery crash will come
To cleanse and shake a wounded hemisphere,
And heal it of a long malignity
That angry time discredits and disowns.
Tonight there are men saying many things;
And some who see life in the last of me
Will answer first the coming call to death;
For death is what is coming, and then life.

I do not say again for the dull sake
Of speech what you have heard me say before,
But rather for the sake of all I am,
And all God made of me. A man to die
As I do must have done some other work
Than man's alone. I was not after glory,
But there was glory with me, like a friend,
Throughout those crippling years when friends were few,
And fearful to be known by their own names
When mine was vilified for their approval.
Yet friends they are, and they did what was given
Their will to do; they could have done no more.
I was the one man mad enough, it seems,
To do my work; and now my work is over.
And you, my dear, are not to mourn for me,
Or for your sons, more than a soul should mourn
In Paradise, done with evil and with earth.
There is not much of earth in what remains
For you; and what there may be left of it
For your endurance you shall have at last
In peace, without the twinge of any fear
For my condition; for I shall be done
With plans and actions that have heretofore
Made your days long and your nights ominous
With darkness and the many distances
That were between us. When the silence comes,
I shall in faith be nearer to you then
Than I am now in fact. What you see now
Is only the outside of an old man,
Older than years have made him. Let him die,
And let him be a thing for little grief.
There was a time for service, and he served;
And there is no more time for anything
But a short gratefulness to those who gave
Their scared allegiance to an enterprise
That has the name of treason — which will serve
As well as any other for the present.
There are some deeds of men that have no names,
And mine may like as not be one of them.
I am not looking far for names tonight.

The King of Glory was without a name
Until men gave him one; yet there He was,
Before we found Him and affronted Him
With numerous ingenuities of evil,
Of which one, with His aid, is to be swept
And washed out of the world with fire and blood.

Once I believed it might have come to pass
With a small cost of blood; but I was dreaming —
Dreaming that I believed. The Voice I heard
When I left you behind me in the north, —
To wait there and to wonder and grow old
Of loneliness, — told only what was best,
And with a saving vagueness, I should know
Till I knew more. And had I known even then —
After grim years of search and suffering,
So many of them to end as they began —
After my sickening doubts and estimations
Of plans abandoned and of new plans vain —
After a weary delving everywhere
For men with every virtue but the Vision —
Could I have known, I say, before I left you
That summer morning, all there was to know —
Even unto the last consuming word
That would have blasted every mortal answer
As lightning would annihilate a leaf,
I might have trembled on that summer morning;
I might have wavered; and I might have failed.

And there are many among men today
To say of me that I had best have wavered.
So has it been, so shall it always be,
For those of us who give ourselves to die
Before we are so parcelled and approved
As to be slaughtered by authority.
We do not make so much of what they say
As they of what our folly says of us;
They give us hardly time enough for that,
And thereby we gain much by losing little.
Few are alive to-day with less to lose

Than I who tell you this, or more to gain;
And whether I speak as one to be destroyed
For no good end outside his own destruction,
Time shall have more to say than men shall hear
Between now and the coming of that harvest
Which is to come. Before it comes, I go —
By the short road that mystery makes long
For man's endurance of accomplishment.
I shall have more to say when I am dead.

The False Gods

"We are false and evanescent, and aware of our deceit,
From the straw that is our vitals to the clay that is our feet.
You may serve us if you must, and you shall have your wage of ashes, —
Though arrears due thereafter may be hard for you to meet.

"You may swear that we are solid, you may say that we are strong,
But we know that we are neither and we say that you are wrong;
You may find an easy worship in acclaiming our indulgence,
But your large admiration of us now is not for long.

"If your doom is to adore us with a doubt that's never still,
And you pray to see our faces — pray in earnest, and you will.
You may gaze at us and live, and live assured of our confusion:
For the False Gods are mortal, and are made for you to kill.

"And you may as well observe, while apprehensively at ease
With an Art that's inorganic and is anything you please,
That anon your newest ruin may lie crumbling unregarded,
Like an old shrine forgotten in a forest of new trees.

"Howsoever like no other be the mode you may employ,
There's an order in the ages for the ages to enjoy;
Though the temples you are shaping and the passions you are singing
Are a long way from Athens and a longer way from Troy.

"When we promise more than ever of what never shall arrive,
And you seem a little more than ordinarily alive,
Make a note that you are sure you understand our obligations —
For there's grief always auditing where two and two are five.

"There was this for us to say and there was this for you to know,
Though it humbles and it hurts us when we have to tell you so.
If you doubt the only truth in all our perjured composition,
May the True Gods attend you and forget us when we go."

Archibald's Example

Old Archibald, in his eternal chair,
Where trespassers, whatever their degree,
Were soon frowned out again, was looking off
Across the clover when he said to me:

"My green hill yonder, where the sun goes down
Without a scratch, was once inhabited
By trees that injured him — an evil trash
That made a cage, and held him while he bled.

"Gone fifty years, I see them as they were
Before they fell. They were a crooked lot
To spoil my sunset, and I saw no time
In fifty years for crooked things to rot.

"Trees, yes; but not a service or a joy
To God or man, for they were thieves of light.
So down they came. Nature and I looked on,
And we were glad when they were out of sight.

"Trees are like men, sometimes; and that being so,
So much for that." He twinkled in his chair,
And looked across the clover to the place
That he remembered when the trees were there.

London Bridge

"Do I hear them? Yes, I hear the children singing — and what of it?
Have you come with eyes afire to find me now and ask me that?
If I were not their father and if you were not their mother,
We might believe they made a noise. … What are you — driving at!"

"Well, be glad that you can hear them, and be glad they are so near us, —
For I have heard the stars of heaven, and they were nearer still.
All within an hour it is that I have heard them calling,
And though I pray for them to cease, I know they never will;
For their music on my heart, though you may freeze it, will fall always,
Like summer snow that never melts upon a mountain-top.
Do you hear them? Do you hear them overhead — the children — singing?
Do you hear the children singing? … God, will you make them stop!"

"And what now in his holy name have you to do with mountains?
We're back to town again, my dear, and we've a dance tonight.
Frozen hearts and falling music? Snow and stars, and — what the devil!
Say it over to me slowly, and be sure you have it right."

"God knows if I be right or wrong in saying what I tell you,
Or if I know the meaning any more of what I say.
All I know is, it will kill me if I try to keep it hidden —
Well, I met him. … Yes, I met him, and I talked with him — today."

"You met him? Did you meet the ghost of someone you had poisoned,
Long ago, before I knew you for the woman that you are?
Take a chair; and don't begin your stories always in the middle.
Was he man, or was he demon? Anyhow, you've gone too far
To go back, and I'm your servant. I'm the lord, but you're the master.
Now go on with what you know, for I'm excited."

       "Do you mean —
Do you mean to make me try to think that you know less than I do?"

"I know that you foreshadow the beginning of a scene.
Pray be careful, and as accurate as if the doors of heaven
Were to swing or to stay bolted from now on for evermore."

"Do you conceive, with all your smooth contempt of every feeling,
Of hiding what you know and what you must have known before?
Is it worth a woman's torture to stand here and have you smiling,
With only your poor fetish of possession on your side?
No thing but one is wholly sure, and that's not one to scare me;
When I meet it I may say to God at last that I have tried.
And yet, for all I know, or all I dare believe, my trials
Henceforward will be more for you to bear than are your own;
And you must give me keys of yours to rooms I have not entered.
Do you see me on your threshold all my life, and there alone?
Will you tell me where you see me in your fancy — when it leads you
Far enough beyond the moment for a glance at the abyss?"

"Will you tell me what intrinsic and amazing sort of nonsense
You are crowding on the patience of the man who gives you — this?
Look around you and be sorry you're not living in an attic,
With a civet and a fish-net, and with you to pay the rent.
I say words that you can spell without the use of all your letters;
And I grant, if you insist, that I've a guess at what you meant."

"Have I told you, then, for nothing, that I met him? Are you trying
To be merry while you try to make me hate you?"

                    "Think again,
My dear, before you tell me, in a language unbecoming
To a lady, what you plan to tell me next. If I complain,
If I seem an atom peevish at the preference you mention —
Or imply, to be precise — you may believe, or you may not,
That I'm a trifle more aware of what he wants than you are.
But I shouldn't throw that at you. Make believe that I forgot.
Make believe that he's a genius, if you like, — but in the meantime
Don't go back to rocking-horses. There, there, there, now."

                    "Make believe!
When you see me standing helpless on a plank above a whirlpool,
Do I drown, or do I hear you when you say it? Make believe?

How much more am I to say or do for you before I tell you
That I met him! What's to follow now may be for you to choose.
Do you hear me? Won't you listen? It's an easy thing to listen.... ."

"And it's easy to be crazy when there's everything to lose."

"If at last you have a notion that I mean what I am saying,
Do I seem to tell you nothing when I tell you I shall try?
If you save me, and I lose him — I don't know — it won't much matter.
I dare say that I've lied enough, but now I do not lie."

"Do you fancy me the one man who has waited and said nothing
While a wife has dragged an old infatuation from a tomb?
Give the thing a little air and it will vanish into ashes.
There you are — piff! presto!"

          "When I came into this room,
It seemed as if I saw the place, and you there at your table,
As you are now at this moment, for the last time in my life;
And I told myself before I came to find you, 'I shall tell him,
If I can, what I have learned of him since I became his wife.'
And if you say, as I've no doubt you will before I finish,
That you have tried unceasingly, with all your might and main,
To teach me, knowing more than I of what it was I needed,
Don't think, with all you may have thought, that you have tried in vain;
For you have taught me more than hides in all the shelves of knowledge
Of how little you found that's in me and was in me all along.
I believed, if I intruded nothing on you that I cared for,
I'd be half as much as horses, — and it seems that I was wrong;
I believed there was enough of earth in me, with all my nonsense
Over things that made you sleepy, to keep something still awake;
But you taught me soon to read my book, and God knows I have read it —
Ages longer than an angel would have read it for your sake.
I have said that you must open other doors than I have entered,
But I wondered while I said it if I might not be obscure.
Is there anything in all your pedigrees and inventories
With a value more elusive than a dollar's? Are you sure
That if I starve another year for you I shall be stronger
To endure another like it — and another — till I'm dead?"

"Has your tame cat sold a picture? — or more likely had a windfall?
Or for God's sake, what's broke loose? Have you a bee-hive in your head?
A little more of this from you will not be easy hearing.
Do you know that? Understand it, if you do; for if you won't. ...
What the devil are you saying! Make believe you never said it,
And I'll say I never heard it. . . . Oh, you. . . . If you. . . ."

"If I don't?"

"There are men who say there's reason hidden somewhere in a woman,
But I doubt if God himself remembers where the key was hung."

"He may not; for they say that even God himself is growing.
I wonder if he makes believe that he is growing young;
I wonder if he makes believe that women who are giving
All they have in holy loathing to a stranger all their lives
Are the wise ones who build houses in the Bible... ."

"Stop — you devil!"

"... Or that souls are any whiter when their bodies are called wives.
If a dollar's worth of gold will hoop the walls of hell together,
Why need heaven be such a ruin of a place that never was?
And if at last I lied my starving soul away to nothing,
Are you sure you might not miss it? Have you come to such a pass
That you would have me longer in your arms if you discovered
That I made you into someone else... . Oh! ... Well, there are worse ways.
But why aim it at my feet — unless you fear you may be sorry. . . .
There are many days ahead of you."

"I do not see those days."

"I can see them. Granted even I am wrong, there are the children.
And are they to praise their father for his insight if we die?
Do you hear them? Do you hear them overhead — the children — singing?
Do you hear them? Do you hear the children?"

"Damn the children!"

"Why?

What have *they* done? … Well, then, — do it… . Do it now, and have it over."

"Oh, you devil! … Oh, you… ."

        "No, I'm not a devil, I'm a prophet —
One who sees the end already of so much that one end more
Would have now the small importance of one other small illusion,
Which in turn would have a welcome where the rest have gone before.
But if I were you, my fancy would look on a little farther
For the glimpse of a release that may be somewhere still in sight.
Furthermore, you must remember those two hundred invitations
For the dancing after dinner. We shall have to shine tonight.
We shall dance, and be as happy as a pair of merry spectres,
On the grave of all the lies that we shall never have to tell;
We shall dance among the ruins of the tomb of our endurance,
And I have not a doubt that we shall do it very well.
There! — I'm glad you've put it back; for I don't like it. Shut the drawer now.
No — no — don't cancel anything. I'll dance until I drop.
I can't walk yet, but I'm going to… . Go away somewhere, and leave me… .
Oh, you children! Oh, you children! … God, will they never stop!"

Tasker Norcross

"Whether all towns and all who live in them —
So long as they be somewhere in this world
That we in our complacency call ours —
Are more or less the same, I leave to you.
I should say less. Whether or not, meanwhile,
We've all two legs — and as for that, we haven't —
There were three kinds of men where I was born:
The good, the not so good, and Tasker Norcross.
Now there are two kinds."

    "Meaning, as I divine,
Your friend is dead," I ventured.

      Ferguson,
Who talked himself at last out of the world
He censured, and is therefore silent now,
Agreed indifferently: "My friends are dead —
Or most of them."

    "Remember one that isn't,"
I said, protesting. "Honor him for his ears;
Treasure him also for his understanding."
Ferguson sighed, and then talked on again:
"You have an overgrown alacrity
For saying nothing much and hearing less;
And I've a thankless wonder, at the start,
How much it is to you that I shall tell
What I have now to say of Tasker Norcross,
And how much to the air that is around you.
But given a patience that is not averse
To the slow tragedies of haunted men —
Horrors, in fact, if you've a skilful eye
To know them at their firesides, or out walking, —"

"Horrors," I said, "are my necessity;
And I would have them, for their best effect,
Always out walking."

　　　Ferguson frowned at me:
"The wisest of us are not those who laugh
Before they know. Most of us never know —
Or the long toil of our mortality
Would not be done. Most of us never know —
And there you have a reason to believe
In God, if you may have no other. Norcross,
Or so I gather of his infirmity,
Was given to know more than he should have known,
And only God knows why. See for yourself
An old house full of ghosts of ancestors,
Who did their best, or worst, and having done it,
Died honorably; and each with a distinction
That hardly would have been for him that had it,
Had honor failed him wholly as a friend.
Honor that is a friend begets a friend.
Whether or not we love him, still we have him;
And we must live somehow by what we have,
Or then we die. If you say chemistry,
Then you must have your molecules in motion,
And in their right abundance. Failing either,
You have not long to dance. Failing a friend,
A genius, or a madness, or a faith
Larger than desperation, you are here
For as much longer than you like as may be.
Imagining now, by way of an example,
Myself a more or less remembered phantom —
Again, I should say less — how many times
A day should I come back to you? No answer.
Forgive me when I seem a little careless,
But we must have examples, or be lucid
Without them; and I question your adherence
To such an undramatic narrative
As this of mine, without the personal hook."

"A time is given in Ecclesiastes
For divers works," I told him. "Is there one
For saying nothing in return for nothing?
If not, there should be." I could feel his eyes,
And they were like two cold inquiring points
Of a sharp metal. When I looked again,
To see them shine, the cold that I had felt
Was gone to make way for a smouldering
Of lonely fire that I, as I knew then,
Could never quench with kindness or with lies.
I should have done whatever there was to do
For Ferguson, yet I could not have mourned
In honesty for once around the clock
The loss of him, for my sake or for his,
Try as I might; nor would his ghost approve,
Had I the power and the unthinking will
To make him tread again without an aim
The road that was behind him — and without
The faith, or friend, or genius, or the madness
That he contended was imperative.

After a silence that had been too long,
"It may be quite as well we don't," he said;
"As well, I mean, that we don't always say it.
You know best what I mean, and I suppose
You might have said it better. What was that?
Incorrigible? Am I incorrigible?
Well, it's a word; and a word has its use,
Or, like a man, it will soon have a grave.
It's a good word enough. Incorrigible,
May be, for all I know, the word for Norcross.
See for yourself that house of his again
That he called home: An old house, painted white,
Square as a box, and chillier than a tomb
To look at or to live in. There were trees —
Too many of them, if such a thing may be —
Before it and around it. Down in front
There was a road, a railroad, and a river;
Then there were hills behind it, and more trees.
The thing would fairly stare at you through trees,

132

Like a pale inmate out of a barred window
With a green shade half down; and I dare say
People who passed have said: 'There's where he lives.
We know him, but we do not seem to know
That we remember any good of him,
Or any evil that is interesting.
There you have all we know and all we care.'
They might have said it in all sorts of ways;
And then, if they perceived a cat, they might
Or might not have remembered what they said.
The cat might have a personality —
And maybe the same one the Lord left out
Of Tasker Norcross, who, for lack of it,
Saw the same sun go down year after year;
All which at last was my discovery.
And only mine, so far as evidence
Enlightens one more darkness. You have known
All round you, all your days, men who are nothing —
Nothing, I mean, so far as time tells yet
Of any other need it has of them
Than to make sextons hardy — but no less
Are to themselves incalculably something,
And therefore to be cherished. God, you see,
Being sorry for them in their fashioning,
Indemnified them with a quaint esteem
Of self, and with illusions long as life.
You know them well, and you have smiled at them;
And they, in their serenity, may have had
Their time to smile at you. Blessed are they
That see themselves for what they never were
Or were to be, and are, for their defect,
At ease with mirrors and the dim remarks
That pass their tranquil ears."

      "Come, come," said I;
"There may be names in your compendium
That we are not yet all on fire for shouting.
Skin most of us of our mediocrity,
We should have nothing then that we could scratch.
The picture smarts. Cover it, if you please,

And do so rather gently. Now for Norcross."

Ferguson closed his eyes in resignation,
While a dead sigh came out of him. "Good God!"
He said, and said it only half aloud,
As if he knew no longer now, nor cared,
If one were there to listen: "Have I said nothing —
Nothing at all — of Norcross? Do you mean
To patronize him till his name becomes
A toy made out of letters? If a name
Is all you need, arrange an honest column
Of all the people you have ever known
That you have never liked. You'll have enough;
And you'll have mine, moreover. No, not yet.
If I assume too many privileges,
I pay, and I alone, for their assumption;
By which, if I assume a darker knowledge
Of Norcross than another, let the weight
Of my injustice aggravate the load
That is not on your shoulders. When I came
To know this fellow Norcross in his house,
I found him as I found him in the street —
No more, no less; indifferent, but no better.
'Worse' were not quite the word: he was not bad;
He was not ... well, he was not anything.
Has your invention ever entertained
The picture of a dusty worm so dry
That even the early bird would shake his head
And fly on farther for another breakfast?"

"But why forget the fortune of the worm,"
I said, "if in the dryness you deplore
Salvation centred and endured? Your Norcross
May have been one for many to have envied."

"Salvation? Fortune? Would the worm say that?
He might; and therefore I dismiss the worm
With all dry things but one. Figures away,
Do you begin to see this man a little?
Do you begin to see him in the air,

With all the vacant horrors of his outline
For you to fill with more than it will hold?
If so, you needn't crown yourself at once
With epic laurel if you seem to fill it.
Horrors, I say, for in the fires and forks
Of a new hell — if one were not enough —
I doubt if a new horror would have held him
With a malignant ingenuity
More to be feared than his before he died.
You smile, as if in doubt. Well, smile again.
Now come into his house, along with me:
The four square sombre things that you see first
Around you are four walls that go as high
As to the ceiling. Norcross knew them well,
And he knew others like them. Fasten to that
With all the claws of your intelligence;
And hold the man before you in his house
As if he were a white rat in a box,
And one that knew himself to be no other.
I tell you twice that he knew all about it,
That you may not forget the worst of all
Our tragedies begin with what we know.
Could Norcross only not have known, I wonder
How many would have blessed and envied him!
Could he have had the usual eye for spots
On others, and for none upon himself,
I smile to ponder on the carriages
That might as well as not have clogged the town
In honor of his end. For there was gold,
You see, though all he needed was a little,
And what he gave said nothing of who gave it.
He would have given it all if in return
There might have been a more sufficient face
To greet him when he shaved. Though you insist
It is the dower, and always, of our degree
Not to be cursed with such invidious insight,
Remember that you stand, you and your fancy,
Now in his house; and since we are together,
See for yourself and tell me what you see.
Tell me the best you see. Make a slight noise

Of recognition when you find a book
That you would not as lief read upside down
As otherwise, for example. If there you fail,
Observe the walls and lead me to the place,
Where you are led. If there you meet a picture
That holds you near it for a longer time
Than you are sorry, you may call it yours,
And hang it in the dark of your remembrance,
Where Norcross never sees. How can he see
That has no eyes to see? And as for music,
He paid with empty wonder for the pangs
Of his infrequent forced endurance of it;
And having had no pleasure, paid no more
For needless immolation, or for the sight
Of those who heard what he was never to hear.
To see them listening was itself enough
To make him suffer; and to watch worn eyes,
On other days, of strangers who forgot
Their sorrows and their failures and themselves
Before a few mysterious odds and ends
Of marble carted from the Parthenon —
And all for seeing what he was never to see,
Because it was alive and he was dead —
Here was a wonder that was more profound
Than any that was in fiddles and brass horns.

"He knew, and in his knowledge there was death.
He knew there was a region all around him
That lay outside man's havoc and affairs,
And yet was not all hostile to their tumult,
Where poets would have served and honored him,
And saved him, had there been anything to save.
But there was nothing, and his tethered range
Was only a small desert. Kings of song
Are not for thrones in deserts. Towers of sound
And flowers of sense are but a waste of heaven
Where there is none to know them from the rocks
And sand-grass of his own monotony
That makes earth less than earth. He could see that,
And he could see no more. The captured light

That may have been or not, for all he cared,
The song that is in sculpture was not his,
But only, to his God-forgotten eyes,
One more immortal nonsense in a world
Where all was mortal, or had best be so,
And so be done with. 'Art,' he would have said,
'Is not life, and must therefore be a lie;'
And with a few profundities like that
He would have controverted and dismissed
The benefit of the Greeks. He had heard of them,
As he had heard of his aspiring soul —
Never to the perceptible advantage,
In his esteem, of either. 'Faith,' he said,
Or would have said if he had thought of it,
'Lives in the same house with Philosophy,
Where the two feed on scraps and are forlorn
As orphans after war. He could see stars,
On a clear night, but he had not an eye
To see beyond them. He could hear spoken words,
But had no ear for silence when alone.
He could eat food of which he knew the savor,
But had no palate for the Bread of Life,
That human desperation, to his thinking,
Made famous long ago, having no other.
Now do you see? Do you begin to see?"

I told him that I did begin to see;
And I was nearer than I should have been
To laughing at his malign inclusiveness,
When I considered that, with all our speed,
We are not laughing yet at funerals.
I see him now as I could see him then,
And I see now that it was good for me,
As it was good for him, that I was quiet;
For Time's eye was on Ferguson, and the shaft
Of its inquiring hesitancy had touched him,
Or so I chose to fancy more than once
Before he told of Norcross. When the word
Of his release (he would have called it so)
Made half an inch of news, there were no tears

That are recorded. Women there may have been
To wish him back, though I should say, not knowing,
The few there were to mourn were not for love,
And were not lovely. Nothing of them, at least,
Was in the meagre legend that I gathered
Years after, when a chance of travel took me
So near the region of his nativity
That a few miles of leisure brought me there;
For there I found a friendly citizen
Who led me to his house among the trees
That were above a railroad and a river.
Square as a box and chillier than a tomb
It was indeed, to look at or to live in —
All which had I been told. "Ferguson died,"
The stranger said, "and then there was an auction.
I live here, but I've never yet been warm.
Remember him? Yes, I remember him.
I knew him — as a man may know a tree —
For twenty years. He may have held himself
A little high when he was here, but now . . .
Yes, I remember Ferguson. Oh, yes."
Others, I found, remembered Ferguson,
But none of them had heard of Tasker Norcross.

A Song at Shannon's

Two men came out of Shannon's having known
The faces of each other for as long
As they had listened there to an old song,
Sung thinly in a wastrel monotone
By some unhappy night-bird, who had flown
Too many times and with a wing too strong
To save himself, and so done heavy wrong
To more frail elements than his alone.

Slowly away they went, leaving behind
More light than was before them. Neither met
The other's eyes again or said a word.
Each to his loneliness or to his kind,
Went his own way, and with his own regret,
Not knowing what the other may have heard.

Souvenir

A vanished house that for an hour I knew
By some forgotten chance when I was young
Had once a glimmering window overhung
With honeysuckle wet with evening dew.
Along the path tall dusky dahlias grew,
And shadowy hydrangeas reached and swung
Ferociously; and over me, among
The moths and mysteries, a blurred bat flew.

Somewhere within there were dim presences
Of days that hovered and of years gone by.
I waited, and between their silences
There was an evanescent faded noise;
And though a child, I knew it was the voice
Of one whose occupation was to die.

Discovery

We told of him as one who should have soared
And seen for us the devastating light
Whereof there is not either day or night,
And shared with us the glamour of the Word
That fell once upon Amos to record
For men at ease in Zion, when the sight
Of ills obscured aggrieved him and the might
Of Hamath was a warning of the Lord.

Assured somehow that he would make us wise,
Our pleasure was to wait; and our surprise
Was hard when we confessed the dry return
Of his regret. For we were still to learn
That earth has not a school where we may go
For wisdom, or for more than we may know.

Firelight

Ten years together without yet a cloud,
They seek each other's eyes at intervals
Of gratefulness to firelight and four walls
For love's obliteration of the crowd.
Serenely and perennially endowed
And bowered as few may be, their joy recalls
No snake, no sword; and over them there falls
The blessing of what neither says aloud.

Wiser for silence, they were not so glad
Were she to read the graven tale of lines
On the wan face of one somewhere alone;
Nor were they more content could he have had
Her thoughts a moment since of one who shines
Apart, and would be hers if he had known.

The New Tenants

The day was here when it was his to know
How fared the barriers he had built between
His triumph and his enemies unseen,
For them to undermine and overthrow;
And it was his no longer to forego
The sight of them, insidious and serene,
Where they were delving always and had been
Left always to be vicious and to grow.

And there were the new tenants who had come,
By doors that were left open unawares,
Into his house, and were so much at home
There now that he would hardly have to guess,
By the slow guile of their vindictiveness,
What ultimate insolence would soon be theirs.

Inferential

Although I saw before me there the face
Of one whom I had honored among men
The least, and on regarding him again
Would not have had him in another place,
He fitted with an unfamiliar grace
The coffin where I could not see him then
As I had seen him and appraised him when
I deemed him unessential to the race.

For there was more of him than what I saw.
And there was on me more than the old awe
That is the common genius of the dead.
I might as well have heard him: "Never mind;
If some of us were not so far behind,
The rest of us were not so far ahead."

The Rat

As often as he let himself be seen
We pitied him, or scorned him, or deplored
The inscrutable profusion of the Lord
Who shaped as one of us a thing so mean —
Who made him human when he might have been
A rat, and so been wholly in accord
With any other creature we abhorred
As always useless and not always clean.

Now he is hiding all alone somewhere,
And in a final hole not ready then;
For now he is among those over there
Who are not coming back to us again.
And we who do the fiction of our share
Say less of rats and rather more of men.

Rahel to Varnhagen

Note. — Rahel Robert and Varnhagen von Ense were married, after many protestations on her part, in 1814. The marriage — so far as he was concerned, at any rate — appears to have been satisfactory.

Now you have read them all; or if not all,
As many as in all conscience I should fancy
To be enough. There are no more of them —
Or none to burn your sleep, or to bring dreams
Of devils. If these are not sufficient, surely
You are a strange young man. I might live on
Alone, and for another forty years,
Or not quite forty, — are you happier now? —
Always to ask if there prevailed elsewhere
Another like yourself that would have held
These aged hands as long as you have held them,
Not once observing, for all I can see,
How they are like your mother's. Well, you have read
His letters now, and you have heard me say
That in them are the cinders of a passion
That was my life; and you have not yet broken
Your way out of my house, out of my sight, —
Into the street. You are a strange young man.
I know as much as that of you, for certain;
And I'm already praying, for your sake,
That you be not too strange. Too much of that
May lead you bye and bye through gloomy lanes
To a sad wilderness, where one may grope
Alone, and always, or until he feels
Ferocious and invisible animals
That wait for men and eat them in the dark.
Why do you sit there on the floor so long,
Smiling at me while I try to be solemn?
Do you not hear it said for your salvation,

When I say truth? Are you, at four and twenty,
So little deceived in us that you interpret
The humor of a woman to be noticed
As her choice between you and Acheron?
Are you so unscathed yet as to infer
That if a woman worries when a man,
Or a man-child, has wet shoes on his feet
She may as well commemorate with ashes
The last eclipse of her tranquillity?
If you look up at me and blink again,
I shall not have to make you tell me lies
To know the letters you have not been reading.
I see now that I may have had for nothing
A most unpleasant shivering in my conscience
When I laid open for your contemplation
The wealth of my worn casket. If I did,
The fault was not yours wholly. Search again
This wreckage we may call for sport a face,
And you may chance upon the price of havoc
That I have paid for a few sorry stones
That shine and have no light — yet once were stars,
And sparkled on a crown. Little and weak
They seem; and they are cold, I fear, for you.
But they that once were fire for me may not
Be cold again for me until I die;
And only God knows if they may be then.
There is a love that ceases to be love
In being ourselves. How, then, are we to lose it?
You that are sure that you know everything
There is to know of love, answer me that.
Well? ... You are not even interested.

Once on a far off time when I was young,
I felt with your assurance, and all through me,
That I had undergone the last and worst
Of love's inventions. There was a boy who brought
The sun with him and woke me up with it,
And that was every morning; every night
I tried to dream of him, but never could,
More than I might have seen in Adam's eyes

Their fond uncertainty when Eve began
The play that all her tireless progeny
Are not yet weary of. One scene of it
Was brief, but was eternal while it lasted;
And that was while I was the happiest
Of an imaginary six or seven,
Somewhere in history but not on earth,
For whom the sky had shaken and let stars
Rain down like diamonds. Then there were clouds,
And a sad end of diamonds; whereupon
Despair came, like a blast that would have brought
Tears to the eyes of all the bears in Finland,
And love was done. That was how much I knew.
Poor little wretch! I wonder where he is
This afternoon. Out of this rain, I hope.

At last, when I had seen so many days
Dressed all alike, and in their marching order,
Go by me that I would not always count them,
One stopped — shattering the whole file of Time,
Or so it seemed; and when I looked again,
There was a man. He struck once with his eyes,
And then there was a woman. I, who had come
To wisdom, or to vision, or what you like,
By the old hidden road that has no name, —
I, who was used to seeing without flying
So much that others fly from without seeing,
Still looked, and was afraid, and looked again.
And after that, when I had read the story
Told in his eyes, and felt within my heart
The bleeding wound of their necessity,
I knew the fear was his. If I had failed him
And flown away from him, I should have lost
Ingloriously my wings in scrambling back,
And found them arms again. If he had struck me
Not only with his eyes but with his hands,
I might have pitied him and hated love,
And then gone mad. I, who have been so strong —
Why don't you laugh? — might even have done all that.
I, who have learned so much, and said so much,

And had the commendations of the great
For one who rules herself — why don't you cry? —
And own a certain small authority
Among the blind, who see no more than ever,
But like my voice, — I would have tossed it all
To Tophet for one man; and he was jealous.
I would have wound a snake around my neck
And then have let it bite me till I died,
If my so doing would have made me sure
That one man might have lived; and he was jealous.
I would have driven these hands into a cage
That held a thousand scorpions, and crushed them,
If only by so poisonous a trial
I could have crushed his doubt. I would have wrung
My living blood with mediaeval engines
Out of my screaming flesh, if only that
Would have made one man sure. I would have paid
For him the tiresome price of body and soul,
And let the lash of a tongue-weary town
Fall as it might upon my blistered name;
And while it fell I could have laughed at it,
Knowing that he had found out finally
Where the wrong was. But there was evil in him
That would have made no more of his possession
Than confirmation of another fault;
And there was honor — if you call it honor
That hoods itself with doubt and wears a crown
Of lead that might as well be gold and fire.
Give it as heavy or as light a name
As any there is that fits. I see myself
Without the power to swear to this or that
That I might be if he had been without it.
Whatever I might have been that I was not,
It only happened that it wasn't so.
Meanwhile, you might seem to be listening:
If you forget yourself and go to sleep,
My treasure, I shall not say this again.
Look up once more into my poor old face,
Where you see beauty, or the Lord knows what,
And say to me aloud what else there is

Than ruins in it that you most admire.

No, there was never anything like that;
Nature has never fastened such a mask
Of radiant and impenetrable merit
On any woman as you say there is
On this one. Not a mask? I thank you, sir,
But you see more with your determination,
I fear, than with your prudence or your conscience;
And you have never met me with my eyes
In all the mirrors I've made faces at.
No, I shall never call you strange again:
You are the young and inconvincible
Epitome of all blind men since Adam.
May the blind lead the blind, if that be so?
And we shall need no mirrors? You are saying
What most I feared you might. But if the blind,
Or one of them, be not so fortunate
As to put out the eyes of recollection,
She might at last, without her meaning it,
Lead on the other, without his knowing it,
Until the two of them should lose themselves
Among dead craters in a lava-field
As empty as a desert on the moon.
I am not speaking in a theatre,
But in a room so real and so familiar
That sometimes I would wreck it. Then I pause,
Remembering there is a King in Weimar —
A monarch, and a poet, and a shepherd
Of all who are astray and are outside
The realm where they should rule. I think of him,
And save the furniture; I think of you,
And am forlorn, finding in you the one
To lavish aspirations and illusions
Upon a faded and forsaken house
Where love, being locked alone, was nigh to burning
House and himself together. Yes, you are strange,
To see in such an injured architecture
Room for new love to live in. Are you laughing?
No? Well, you are not crying, as you should be.

Tears, even if they told only gratitude
For your escape, and had no other story,
Were surely more becoming than a smile
For my unwomanly straightforwardness
In seeing for you, through my close gate of years
Your forty ways to freedom. Why do you smile?
And while I'm trembling at my faith in you
In giving you to read this book of danger
That only one man living might have written —
These letters, which have been a part of me
So long that you may read them all again
As often as you look into my face,
And hear them when I speak to you, and feel them
Whenever you have to touch me with your hand, —
Why are you so unwilling to be spared?
Why do you still believe in me? But no,
I'll find another way to ask you that.
I wonder if there is another way
That says it better, and means anything.
There is no other way that could be worse?
I was not asking you; it was myself
Alone that I was asking. Why do I dip
For lies, when there is nothing in my well
But shining truth, you say? How do you know?
Truth has a lonely life down where she lives;
And many a time, when she comes up to breathe,
She sinks before we seize her, and makes ripples.
Possibly you may know no more of me
Than a few ripples; and they may soon be gone,
Leaving you then with all my shining truth
Drowned in a shining water; and when you look
You may not see me there, but something else
That never was a woman — being yourself.
You say to me my truth is past all drowning,
And safe with you for ever? You know all that?
How do you know all that, and who has told you?
You know so much that I'm an atom frightened
Because you know so little. And what is this?
You know the luxury there is in haunting
The blasted thoroughfares of disillusion —

If that's your name for them — with only ghosts
For company? You know that when a woman
Is blessed, or cursed, with a divine impatience
(Another name of yours for a bad temper)
She must have one at hand on whom to wreak it
(That's what you mean, whatever the turn you give it),
Sure of a kindred sympathy, and thereby
Effect a mutual calm? You know that wisdom,
Given in vain to make a food for those
Who are without it, will be seen at last,
And even at last only by those who gave it,
As one or more of the forgotten crumbs
That others leave? You know that men's applause
And women's envy savor so much of dust
That I go hungry, having at home no fare
But the same changeless bread that I may swallow
Only with tears and prayers? Who told you that?
You know that if I read, and read alone,
Too many books that no men yet have written,
I may go blind, or worse? You know yourself,
Of all insistent and insidious creatures,
To be the one to save me, and to guard
For me their flaming language? And you know
That if I give much headway to the whim
That's in me never to be quite sure that even
Through all those years of storm and fire I waited
For this one rainy day, I may go on,
And on, and on alone, through smoke and ashes,
To a cold end? You know so dismal much
As that about me? ... Well, I believe you do.

Nimmo

Since you remember Nimmo, and arrive
At such a false and florid and far drawn
Confusion of odd nonsense, I connive
No longer, though I may have led you on.

So much is told and heard and told again,
So many with his legend are engrossed,
That I, more sorry now than I was then,
May live on to be sorry for his ghost.

You knew him, and you must have known his eyes, —
How deep they were, and what a velvet light
Came out of them when anger or surprise,
Or laughter, or Francesca, made them bright.

No, you will not forget such eyes, I think, —
And you say nothing of them. Very well.
I wonder if all history's worth a wink,
Sometimes, or if my tale be one to tell.

For they began to lose their velvet light;
Their fire grew dead without and small within;
And many of you deplored the needless fight
That somewhere in the dark there must have been.

All fights are needless, when they're not our own,
But Nimmo and Francesca never fought.
Remember that; and when you are alone,
Remember me — and think what I have thought.

Now, mind you, I say nothing of what was,
Or never was, or could or could not be:
Bring not suspicion's candle to the glass
That mirrors a friend's face to memory.

Of what you see, see all, — but see no more;
For what I show you here will not be there.
The devil has had his way with paint before,
And he's an artist, — and you needn't stare.

There was a painter and he painted well:
He'd paint you Daniel in the lions' den,
Beelzebub, Elaine, or William Tell.
I'm coming back to Nimmo's eyes again.

The painter put the devil in those eyes,
Unless the devil did, and there he stayed;
And then the lady fled from paradise,
And there's your fact. The lady was afraid.

She must have been afraid, or may have been,
Of evil in their velvet all the while;
But sure as I'm a sinner with a skin,
I'll trust the man as long as he can smile.

I trust him who can smile and then may live
In my heart's house, where Nimmo is today.
God knows if I have more than men forgive
To tell him; but I played, and I shall pay.

I knew him then, and if I know him yet,
I know in him, defeated and estranged,
The calm of men forbidden to forget
The calm of women who have loved and changed.

But there are ways that are beyond our ways,
Or he would not be calm and she be mute,
As one by one their lost and empty days
Pass without even the warmth of a dispute.

God help us all when women think they see;
God save us when they do. I'm fair; but though
I know him only as he looks to me,
I know him, — and I tell Francesca so.

And what of Nimmo? Little would you ask
Of him, could you but see him as I can,
At his bewildered and unfruitful task
Of being what he was born to be — a man.

Better forget that I said anything
Of what your tortured memory may disclose;
I know him, and your worst remembering
Would count as much as nothing, I suppose.

Meanwhile, I trust him; and I know his way
Of trusting me, as always in his youth.
I'm painting here a better man, you say,
Than I, the painter; and you say the truth.

Peace on Earth

He took a frayed hat from his head,
And "Peace on Earth" was what he said.
"A morsel out of what you're worth,
And there we have it: Peace on Earth.
Not much, although a little more
Than what there was on earth before.
I'm as you see, I'm Ichabod, —
But never mind the ways I've trod;
I'm sober now, so help me God."

I could not pass the fellow by.
"Do you believe in God?" said I;
"And is there to be Peace on Earth?"

"Tonight we celebrate the birth,"
He said, "of One who died for men;
The Son of God, we say. What then?
Your God, or mine? I'd make you laugh
Were I to tell you even half
That I have learned of mine today
Where yours would hardly seem to stay.
Could He but follow in and out
Some anthropoids I know about,
The God to whom you may have prayed
Might see a world He never made."

"Your words are flowing full," said I;
"But yet they give me no reply;
Your fountain might as well be dry."

"A wiser One than you, my friend,
Would wait and hear me to the end;
And for His eyes a light would shine
Through this unpleasant shell of mine

That in your fancy makes of me
A Christmas curiosity.
All right, I might be worse than that;
And you might now be lying flat;
I might have done it from behind,
And taken what there was to find.
Don't worry, for I'm not that kind.
'Do I believe in God?' Is that
The price tonight of a new hat?
Has He commanded that His name
Be written everywhere the same?
Have all who live in every place
Identified His hidden face?
Who knows but He may like as well
My story as one you may tell?
And if He show me there be Peace
On Earth, as there be fields and trees
Outside a jail-yard, am I wrong
If now I sing Him a new song?
Your world is in yourself, my friend,
For your endurance to the end;
And all the Peace there is on Earth
Is faith in what your world is worth,
And saying, without any lies,
Your world could not be otherwise."

"One might say that and then be shot,"
I told him; and he said: "Why not?"
I ceased, and gave him rather more
Than he was counting of my store.
"And since I have it, thanks to you,
Don't ask me what I mean to do,"
Said he. "Believe that even I
Would rather tell the truth than lie —
On Christmas Eve. No matter why."

His unshaved, educated face,
His inextinguishable grace,
And his hard smile, are with me still,
Deplore the vision as I will;

For whatsoever he be at,
So droll a derelict as that
Should have at least another hat.

Late Summer

(Alcaics)

Confused, he found her lavishing feminine
Gold upon clay, and found her inscrutable;
 And yet she smiled. Why, then, should horrors
Be as they were, without end, her playthings?

And why were dead years hungrily telling her
Lies of the dead, who told them again to her?
 If now she knew, there might be kindness
Clamoring yet where a faith lay stifled.

A little faith in him, and the ruinous
Past would be for time to annihilate,
 And wash out, like a tide that washes
Out of the sand what a child has drawn there.

God, what a shining handful of happiness,
Made out of days and out of eternities,
 Were now the pulsing end of patience —
Could he but have what a ghost had stolen!

What was a man before him, or ten of them,
While he was here alive who could answer them,
 And in their teeth fling confirmations
Harder than agates against an egg-shell?

But now the man was dead, and would come again
Never, though she might honor ineffably
 The flimsy wraith of him she conjured
Out of a dream with his wand of absence.

And if the truth were now but a mummery,
Meriting pride's implacable irony,

So much the worse for pride. Moreover,
Save her or fail, there was conscience always.

Meanwhile, a few misgivings of innocence,
Imploring to be sheltered and credited,
 Were not amiss when she revealed them.
Whether she struggled or not, he saw them.

Also, he saw that while she was hearing him
Her eyes had more and more of the past in them;
 And while he told what cautious honor
Told him was all he had best be sure of,

He wondered once or twice, inadvertently,
Where shifting winds were driving his argosies,
 Long anchored and as long unladen,
Over the foam for the golden chances.

"If men were not for killing so carelessly,
And women were for wiser endurances,"
 He said, "we might have yet a world here
Fitter for Truth to be seen abroad in;

"If Truth were not so strange in her nakedness,
And we were less forbidden to look at it,
 We might not have to look." He stared then
Down at the sand where the tide threw forward

Its cold, unconquered lines, that unceasingly
Foamed against hope, and fell. He was calm enough,
 Although he knew he might be silenced
Out of all calm; and the night was coming.

"I climb for you the peak of his infamy
That you may choose your fall if you cling to it.
 No more for me unless you say more.
All you have left of a dream defends you:

"The truth may be as evil an augury
As it was needful now for the two of us.

160

We cannot have the dead between us.
Tell me to go, and I go." — She pondered:

"What you believe is right for the two of us
Makes it as right that you are not one of us.
 If this be needful truth you tell me,
Spare me, and let me have lies hereafter."

She gazed away where shadows were covering
The whole cold ocean's healing indifference.
 No ship was coming. When the darkness
Fell, she was there, and alone, still gazing.

An Evangelist's Wife

"Why am I not myself these many days,
You ask? And have you nothing more to ask?
I do you wrong? I do not hear your praise
To God for giving you me to share your task?

"Jealous — of Her? Because her cheeks are pink,
And she has eyes? No, not if she had seven.
If you should only steal an hour to think,
Sometime, there might be less to be forgiven.

"No, you are never cruel. If once or twice
I found you so, I could applaud and sing.
Jealous of — What? You are not very wise.
Does not the good Book tell you anything?

"In David's time poor Michal had to go.
Jealous of God? Well, if you like it so."

The Old King's New Jester

You that in vain would front the coming order
With eyes that meet forlornly what they must,
And only with a furtive recognition
See dust where there is dust, —
Be sure you like it always in your faces,
Obscuring your best graces,
Blinding your speech and sight,
Before you seek again your dusty places
Where the old wrong seems right.

Longer ago than cave-men had their changes
Our fathers may have slain a son or two,
Discouraging a further dialectic
Regarding what was new;
And after their unstudied admonition
Occasional contrition
For their old-fashioned ways
May have reduced their doubts, and in addition
Softened their final days.

Farther away than feet shall ever travel
Are the vague towers of our unbuilded State;
But there are mightier things than we to lead us,
That will not let us wait.
And we go on with none to tell us whether
Or not we've each a tether
Determining how fast or far we go;
And it is well, since we must go together,
That we are not to know.

If the old wrong and all its injured glamour
Haunts you by day and gives your night no peace,
You may as well, agreeably and serenely,
Give the new wrong its lease;

For should you nourish a too fervid yearning
For what is not returning,
The vicious and unfused ingredient
May give you qualms — and one or two concerning
The last of your content.

Lazarus

"No, Mary, there was nothing — not a word.
Nothing, and always nothing. Go again
Yourself, and he may listen — or at least
Look up at you, and let you see his eyes.
I might as well have been the sound of rain,
A wind among the cedars, or a bird;
Or nothing. Mary, make him look at you;
And even if he should say that we are nothing,
To know that you have heard him will be something.
And yet he loved us, and it was for love
The Master gave him back. Why did He wait
So long before He came? Why did He weep?
I thought He would be glad — and Lazarus —
To see us all again as He had left us —
All as it was, all as it was before."

Mary, who felt her sister's frightened arms
Like those of someone drowning who had seized her,
Fearing at last they were to fail and sink
Together in this fog-stricken sea of strangeness,
Fought sadly, with bereaved indignant eyes,
To find again the fading shores of home
That she had seen but now could see no longer.
Now she could only gaze into the twilight,
And in the dimness know that he was there,
Like someone that was not. He who had been
Their brother, and was dead, now seemed alive
Only in death again — or worse than death;
For tombs at least, always until today,
Though sad were certain. There was nothing certain
For man or God in such a day as this;
For there they were alone, and there was he —
Alone; and somewhere out of Bethany,
The Master — who had come to them so late,

Only for love of them and then so slowly,
And was for their sake hunted now by men
Who feared Him as they feared no other prey —
For the world's sake was hidden. "Better the tomb
For Lazarus than life, if this be life,"
She thought; and then to Martha, "No, my dear,"
She said aloud; "not as it was before.
Nothing is ever as it was before,
Where Time has been. Here there is more than Time;
And we that are so lonely and so far
From home, since he is with us here again,
Are farther now from him and from ourselves
Than we are from the stars. He will not speak
Until the spirit that is in him speaks;
And we must wait for all we are to know,
Or even to learn that we are not to know.
Martha, we are too near to this for knowledge,
And that is why it is that we must wait.
Our friends are coming if we call for them,
And there are covers we'll put over him
To make him warmer. We are too young, perhaps,
To say that we know better what is best
Than he. We do not know how old he is.
If you remember what the Master said,
Try to believe that we need have no fear.
Let me, the selfish and the careless one,
Be housewife and a mother for tonight;
For I am not so fearful as you are,
And I was not so eager."

     Martha sank
Down at her sister's feet and there sat watching
A flower that had a small familiar name
That was as old as memory, but was not
The name of what she saw now in its brief
And infinite mystery that so frightened her
That life became a terror. Tears again
Flooded her eyes and overflowed. "No, Mary,"
She murmured slowly, hating her own words
Before she heard them, "you are not so eager

To see our brother as we see him now;
Neither is He who gave him back to us.
I was to be the simple one, as always,
And this was all for me." She stared again
Over among the trees where Lazarus,
Who seemed to be a man who was not there,
Might have been one more shadow among shadows,
If she had not remembered. Then she felt
The cool calm hands of Mary on her face,
And shivered, wondering if such hands were real.

"The Master loved you as He loved us all,
Martha; and you are saying only things
That children say when they have had no sleep.
Try somehow now to rest a little while;
You know that I am here, and that our friends
Are coming if I call."

      Martha at last
Arose, and went with Mary to the door,
Where they stood looking off at the same place,
And at the same shape that was always there
As if it would not ever move or speak,
And always would be there. "Mary, go now,
Before the dark that will be coming hides him.
I am afraid of him out there alone,
Unless I see him; and I have forgotten
What sleep is. Go now — make him look at you —
And I shall hear him if he stirs or whispers.
Go! — or I'll scream and bring all Bethany
To come and make him speak. Make him say once
That he is glad, and God may say the rest.
Though He say I shall sleep, and sleep for ever,
I shall not care for that ... Go!"

      Mary, moving
Almost as if an angry child had pushed her,
Went forward a few steps; and having waited
As long as Martha's eyes would look at hers,
Went forward a few more, and a few more;

And so, until she came to Lazarus,
Who crouched with his face hidden in his hands,
Like one that had no face. Before she spoke,
Feeling her sister's eyes that were behind her
As if the door where Martha stood were now
As far from her as Egypt, Mary turned
Once more to see that she was there. Then, softly,
Fearing him not so much as wondering
What his first word might be, said, "Lazarus,
Forgive us if we seemed afraid of you;"
And having spoken, pitied her poor speech
That had so little seeming gladness in it,
So little comfort, and so little love.

There was no sign from him that he had heard,
Or that he knew that she was there, or cared
Whether she spoke to him again or died
There at his feet. "We love you, Lazarus,
And we are not afraid. The Master said
We need not be afraid. Will you not say
To me that you are glad? Look, Lazarus!
Look at my face, and see me. This is Mary."

She found his hands and held them. They were cool,
Like hers, but they were not so calm as hers.
Through the white robes in which his friends had wrapped him
When he had groped out of that awful sleep,
She felt him trembling and she was afraid.
At last he sighed; and she prayed hungrily
To God that she might have again the voice
Of Lazarus, whose hands were giving her now
The recognition of a living pressure
That was almost a language. When he spoke,
Only one word that she had waited for
Came from his lips, and that word was her name.

"I heard them saying, Mary, that He wept
Before I woke." The words were low and shaken,
Yet Mary knew that he who uttered them
Was Lazarus; and that would be enough

Until there should be more … "Who made Him come,
That He should weep for me? … Was it you, Mary?"
The questions held in his incredulous eyes
Were more than she would see. She looked away;
But she had felt them and should feel for ever,
She thought, their cold and lonely desperation
That had the bitterness of all cold things
That were not cruel. "I should have wept," he said,
"If I had been the Master…. ."

      Now she could feel
His hands above her hair — the same black hair
That once he made a jest of, praising it,
While Martha's busy eyes had left their work
To flash with laughing envy. Nothing of that
Was to be theirs again; and such a thought
Was like the flying by of a quick bird
Seen through a shadowy doorway in the twilight.
For now she felt his hands upon her head,
Like weights of kindness: "I forgive you, Mary…. .
You did not know — Martha could not have known —
Only the Master knew…. . Where is He now?
Yes, I remember. They came after Him.
May the good God forgive Him. . . . I forgive Him.
I must; and I may know only from Him
The burden of all this…. . Martha was here —
But I was not yet here. She was afraid…. .
Why did He do it, Mary? Was it — you?
Was it for you? … Where are the friends I saw?
Yes, I remember. They all went away.
I made them go away…. Where is He now? …
What do I see down there? Do I see Martha —
Down by the door? … I must have time for this."

Lazarus looked about him fearfully,
And then again at Mary, who discovered
Awakening apprehension in his eyes,
And shivered at his feet. All she had feared
Was here; and only in the slow reproach
Of his forgiveness lived his gratitude.

Why had he asked if it was all for her
That he was here? And what had Martha meant?
Why had the Master waited? What was coming
To Lazarus, and to them, that had not come?
What had the Master seen before He came,
That He had come so late?

      "Where is He, Mary?"
Lazarus asked again. "Where did He go?"
Once more he gazed about him, and once more
At Mary for an answer. "Have they found Him?
Or did He go away because He wished
Never to look into my eyes again? ...
That, I could understand.... Where is He, Mary?"

"I do not know," she said. "Yet in my heart
I know that He is living, as you are living —
Living, and here. He is not far from us.
He will come back to us and find us all —
Lazarus, Martha, Mary — everything —
All as it was before. Martha said that.
And He said we were not to be afraid."
Lazarus closed his eyes while on his face
A tortured adumbration of a smile
Flickered an instant. "All as it was before,"
He murmured wearily. "Martha said that;
And He said you were not to be afraid . . .
Not you ... Not you ... Why should you be afraid?
Give all your little fears, and Martha's with them,
To me; and I will add them unto mine,
Like a few rain-drops to Gennesaret."

"If you had frightened me in other ways,
Not willing it," Mary said, "I should have known
You still for Lazarus. But who is this?
Tell me again that you are Lazarus;
And tell me if the Master gave to you
No sign of a new joy that shall be coming
To this house that He loved. Are you afraid?
Are you afraid, who have felt everything —

And seen … ?"

But Lazarus only shook his head,
Staring with his bewildered shining eyes
Hard into Mary's face. "I do not know,
Mary," he said, after a long time.
"When I came back, I knew the Master's eyes
Were looking into mine. I looked at His,
And there was more in them than I could see.
At first I could see nothing but His eyes;
Nothing else anywhere was to be seen —
Only His eyes. And they looked into mine —
Long into mine, Mary, as if He knew."

Mary began to be afraid of words
As she had never been afraid before
Of loneliness or darkness, or of death,
But now she must have more of them or die:
"He cannot know that there is worse than death,"
She said. "And you …"

"Yes, there is worse than death."
Said Lazarus; "and that was what He knew;
And that is what it was that I could see
This morning in his eyes. I was afraid,
But not as you are. There is worse than death,
Mary; and there is nothing that is good
For you in dying while you are still here.
Mary, never go back to that again.
You would not hear me if I told you more,
For I should say it only in a language
That you are not to learn by going back.
To be a child again is to go forward —
And that is much to know. Many grow old,
And fade, and go away, not knowing how much
That is to know. Mary, the night is coming,
And there will soon be darkness all around you.
Let us go down where Martha waits for us,
And let there be light shining in this house."

He rose, but Mary would not let him go:
"Martha, when she came back from here, said only
That she heard nothing. And have you no more
For Mary now than you had then for Martha?
Is Nothing, Lazarus, all you have for me?
Was Nothing all you found where you have been?
If that be so, what is there worse than that —
Or better — if that be so? And why should you,
With even our love, go the same dark road over?"

"I could not answer that, if that were so,"
Said Lazarus, — "not even if I were God.
Why should He care whether I came or stayed,
If that were so? Why should the Master weep —
For me, or for the world, — or save Himself
Longer for nothing? And if that were so,
Why should a few years' more mortality
Make Him a fugitive where flight were needless,
Had He but held his peace and given his nod
To an old Law that would be new as any?
I cannot say the answer to all that;
Though I may say that He is not afraid,
And that it is not for the joy there is
In serving an eternal Ignorance
Of our futility that He is here.
Is that what you and Martha mean by Nothing?
Is that what you are fearing? If that be so,
There are more weeds than lentils in your garden.
And one whose weeds are laughing at his harvest
May as well have no garden; for not there
Shall he be gleaning the few bits and orts
Of life that are to save him. For my part,
I am again with you, here among shadows
That will not always be so dark as this;
Though now I see there's yet an evil in me
That made me let you be afraid of me.
No, I was not afraid — not even of life.
I thought I was … I must have time for this;
And all the time there is will not be long.
I cannot tell you what the Master saw

This morning in my eyes. I do not know.
I cannot yet say how far I have gone,
Or why it is that I am here again,
Or where the old road leads. I do not know.
I know that when I did come back, I saw
His eyes again among the trees and faces —
Only His eyes; and they looked into mine —
Long into mine — long, long, as if He knew."

The Man against the Sky

To

the memory of

WILLIAM EDWARD BUTLER

Flammonde

The man Flammonde, from God knows where,
With firm address and foreign air,
With news of nations in his talk
And something royal in his walk,
With glint of iron in his eyes,
But never doubt, nor yet surprise,
Appeared, and stayed, and held his head
As one by kings accredited.

Erect, with his alert repose
About him, and about his clothes,
He pictured all tradition hears
Of what we owe to fifty years.
His cleansing heritage of taste
Paraded neither want nor waste;
And what he needed for his fee
To live, he borrowed graciously.

He never told us what he was,
Or what mischance, or other cause,
Had banished him from better days
To play the Prince of Castaways.

Meanwhile he played surpassing well
A part, for most, unplayable;
In fine, one pauses, half afraid
To say for certain that he played.

For that, one may as well forego
Conviction as to yes or no;
Nor can I say just how intense
Would then have been the difference
To several, who, having striven
In vain to get what he was given,
Would see the stranger taken on
By friends not easy to be won.

Moreover, many a malcontent
He soothed and found munificent;
His courtesy beguiled and foiled
Suspicion that his years were soiled;
His mien distinguished any crowd,
His credit strengthened when he bowed;
And women, young and old, were fond
Of looking at the man Flammonde.

There was a woman in our town
On whom the fashion was to frown;
But while our talk renewed the tinge
Of a long-faded scarlet fringe,
The man Flammonde saw none of that,
And what he saw we wondered at —
That none of us, in her distress,
Could hide or find our littleness.

There was a boy that all agreed
Had shut within him the rare seed
Of learning. We could understand,
But none of us could lift a hand.
The man Flammonde appraised the youth,
And told a few of us the truth;
And thereby, for a little gold,
A flowered future was unrolled.

There were two citizens who fought
For years and years, and over nought;
They made life awkward for their friends,
And shortened their own dividends.
The man Flammonde said what was wrong
Should be made right; nor was it long
Before they were again in line,
And had each other in to dine.

And these I mention are but four
Of many out of many more.
So much for them. But what of him —
So firm in every look and limb?
What small satanic sort of kink
Was in his brain? What broken link
Withheld him from the destinies
That came so near to being his?

What was he, when we came to sift
His meaning, and to note the drift
Of incommunicable ways
That make us ponder while we praise?
Why was it that his charm revealed
Somehow the surface of a shield?
What was it that we never caught?
What was he, and what was he not?

How much it was of him we met
We cannot ever know; nor yet
Shall all he gave us quite atone
For what was his, and his alone;
Nor need we now, since he knew best,
Nourish an ethical unrest:
Rarely at once will nature give
The power to be Flammonde and live.

We cannot know how much we learn
From those who never will return,
Until a flash of unforeseen

Remembrance falls on what has been.
We've each a darkening hill to climb;
And this is why, from time to time
In Tilbury Town, we look beyond
Horizons for the man Flammonde.

The Gift of God

Blessed with a joy that only she
Of all alive shall ever know,
She wears a proud humility
For what it was that willed it so, —
That her degree should be so great
Among the favored of the Lord
That she may scarcely bear the weight
Of her bewildering reward.

As one apart, immune, alone,
Or featured for the shining ones,
And like to none that she has known
Of other women's other sons, —
The firm fruition of her need,
He shines anointed; and he blurs
Her vision, till it seems indeed
A sacrilege to call him hers.

She fears a little for so much
Of what is best, and hardly dares
To think of him as one to touch
With aches, indignities, and cares;
She sees him rather at the goal,
Still shining; and her dream foretells
The proper shining of a soul
Where nothing ordinary dwells.

Perchance a canvass of the town
Would find him far from flags and shouts,
And leave him only the renown
Of many smiles and many doubts;
Perchance the crude and common tongue
Would havoc strangely with his worth;
But she, with innocence unwrung,

Would read his name around the earth.

And others, knowing how this youth
Would shine, if love could make him great,
When caught and tortured for the truth
Would only writhe and hesitate;
While she, arranging for his days
What centuries could not fulfill,
Transmutes him with her faith and praise,
And has him shining where she will.

She crowns him with her gratefulness,
And says again that life is good;
And should the gift of God be less
In him than in her motherhood,
His fame, though vague, will not be small,
As upward through her dream he fares,
Half clouded with a crimson fall
Of roses thrown on marble stairs.
The Clinging Vine

"Be calm? And was I frantic?
  You'll have me laughing soon.
I'm calm as this Atlantic,
  And quiet as the moon;
I may have spoken faster
  Than once, in other days;
For I've no more a master,
  And now — 'Be calm,' he says.

"Fear not, fear no commotion, —
  I'll be as rocks and sand;
The moon and stars and ocean
  Will envy my command;
No creature could be stiller
  In any kind of place
Than I ... No, I'll not kill her;
  Her death is in her face.

"Be happy while she has it,

For she'll not have it long;
 A year, and then you'll pass it,
 Preparing a new song.
And I'm a fool for prating
 Of what a year may bring,
When more like her are waiting
 For more like you to sing.

"You mock me with denial,
 You mean to call me hard?
You see no room for trial
 When all my doors are barred?
You say, and you'd say dying,
 That I dream what I know;
And sighing, and denying,
 You'd hold my hand and go.

"You scowl — and I don't wonder;
 I spoke too fast again;
But you'll forgive one blunder,
 For you are like most men:
You are, — or so you've told me,
 So many mortal times,
That heaven ought not to hold me
 Accountable for crimes.

"Be calm? Was I unpleasant?
 Then I'll be more discreet,
And grant you, for the present,
 The balm of my defeat:
What she, with all her striving,
 Could not have brought about,
You've done. Your own contriving
 Has put the last light out.

"If she were the whole story,
 If worse were not behind,
I'd creep with you to glory,
 Believing I was blind;
I'd creep, and go on seeming

To be what I despise.
You laugh, and say I'm dreaming,
And all your laughs are lies.

"Are women mad? A few are,
And if it's true you say —
If most men are as you are —
We'll all be mad some day.
Be calm — and let me finish;
There's more for you to know.
I'll talk while you diminish,
And listen while you grow.

"There was a man who married
Because he couldn't see;
And all his days he carried
The mark of his degree.
But you — you came clear-sighted,
And found truth in my eyes;
And all my wrongs you've righted
With lies, and lies, and lies.

"You've killed the last assurance
That once would have me strive
To rouse an old endurance
That is no more alive.
It makes two people chilly
To say what we have said,
But you — you'll not be silly
And wrangle for the dead.

"You don't? You never wrangle?
Why scold then, — or complain?
More words will only mangle
What you've already slain.
Your pride you can't surrender?
My name — for that you fear?
Since when were men so tender,
And honor so severe?

"No more — I'll never bear it.
 I'm going. I'm like ice.
My burden? You would share it?
 Forbid the sacrifice!
Forget so quaint a notion,
 And let no more be told;
For moon and stars and ocean
 And you and I are cold."
Cassandra

I heard one who said: "Verily,
 What word have I for children here?
Your Dollar is your only Word,
 The wrath of it your only fear.

"You build it altars tall enough
 To make you see, but you are blind;
You cannot leave it long enough
 To look before you or behind.

"When Reason beckons you to pause,
 You laugh and say that you know best;
But what it is you know, you keep
 As dark as ingots in a chest.

"You laugh and answer, 'We are young;
 O leave us now, and let us grow.' —
Not asking how much more of this
 Will Time endure or Fate bestow.

"Because a few complacent years
 Have made your peril of your pride,
Think you that you are to go on
 Forever pampered and untried?

"What lost eclipse of history,
 What bivouac of the marching stars,
Has given the sign for you to see
 Millenniums and last great wars?

"What unrecorded overthrow
 Of all the world has ever known,
Or ever been, has made itself
 So plain to you, and you alone?

"Your Dollar, Dove and Eagle make
 A Trinity that even you
Rate higher than you rate yourselves;
 It pays, it flatters, and it's new.

"And though your very flesh and blood
 Be what your Eagle eats and drinks,
You'll praise him for the best of birds,
 Not knowing what the Eagle thinks.

"The power is yours, but not the sight;
 You see not upon what you tread;
You have the ages for your guide,
 But not the wisdom to be led.

"Think you to tread forever down
 The merciless old verities?
And are you never to have eyes
 To see the world for what it is?

"Are you to pay for what you have
 With all you are?" — No other word
We caught, but with a laughing crowd
 Moved on. None heeded, and few heard.

John Gorham

"Tell me what you're doing over here, John Gorham,
Sighing hard and seeming to be sorry when you're not;
Make me laugh or let me go now, for long faces in the moonlight
Are a sign for me to say again a word that you forgot." —

"I'm over here to tell you what the moon already
May have said or maybe shouted ever since a year ago;
I'm over here to tell you what you are, Jane Wayland,
And to make you rather sorry, I should say, for being so." —

"Tell me what you're saying to me now, John Gorham,
Or you'll never see as much of me as ribbons any more;
I'll vanish in as many ways as I have toes and fingers,
And you'll not follow far for one where flocks have been before." —

"I'm sorry now you never saw the flocks, Jane Wayland,
But you're the one to make of them as many as you need.
And then about the vanishing. It's I who mean to vanish;
And when I'm here no longer you'll be done with me indeed." —

"That's a way to tell me what I am, John Gorham!
How am I to know myself until I make you smile?
Try to look as if the moon were making faces at you,
And a little more as if you meant to stay a little while." —

"You are what it is that over rose-blown gardens
Makes a pretty flutter for a season in the sun;
You are what it is that with a mouse, Jane Wayland,
Catches him and lets him go and eats him up for fun." —

"Sure I never took you for a mouse, John Gorham;
All you say is easy, but so far from being true
That I wish you wouldn't ever be again the one to think so;
For it isn't cats and butterflies that I would be to you." —

"All your little animals are in one picture —
One I've had before me since a year ago to-night;
And the picture where they live will be of you, Jane Wayland,
Till you find a way to kill them or to keep them out of sight." —

"Won't you ever see me as I am, John Gorham,
Leaving out the foolishness and all I never meant?
Somewhere in me there's a woman, if you know the way to find her.
Will you like me any better if I prove it and repent?"

"I doubt if I shall ever have the time, Jane Wayland;
And I dare say all this moonlight lying round us might as well
Fall for nothing on the shards of broken urns that are forgotten,
As on two that have no longer much of anything to tell."

Stafford's Cabin

Once there was a cabin here, and once there was a man;
And something happened here before my memory began.
Time has made the two of them the fuel of one flame
And all we have of them is now a legend and a name.

All I have to say is what an old man said to me,
And that would seem to be as much as there will ever be.
"Fifty years ago it was we found it where it sat." —
And forty years ago it was old Archibald said that.

"An apple tree that's yet alive saw something, I suppose,
Of what it was that happened there, and what no mortal knows.
Some one on the mountain heard far off a master shriek,
And then there was a light that showed the way for men to seek.

"We found it in the morning with an iron bar behind,
And there were chains around it; but no search could ever find,
Either in the ashes that were left, or anywhere,
A sign to tell of who or what had been with Stafford there.

"Stafford was a likely man with ideas of his own —
Though I could never like the kind that likes to live alone;
And when you met, you found his eyes were always on your shoes,
As if they did the talking when he asked you for the news.

"That's all, my son. Were I to talk for half a hundred years
I'd never clear away from there the cloud that never clears.
We buried what was left of it, — the bar, too, and the chains;
And only for the apple tree there's nothing that remains."

Forty years ago it was I heard the old man say,
"That's all, my son." — And here again I find the place to-day,
Deserted and told only by the tree that knows the most,
And overgrown with golden-rod as if there were no ghost.

Hillcrest

To Mrs. Edward MacDowell

No sound of any storm that shakes
Old island walls with older seas
Comes here where now September makes
An island in a sea of trees.

Between the sunlight and the shade
A man may learn till he forgets
The roaring of a world remade,
And all his ruins and regrets;

And if he still remembers here
Poor fights he may have won or lost, —
If he be ridden with the fear
Of what some other fight may cost, —

If, eager to confuse too soon,
What he has known with what may be,
He reads a planet out of tune
For cause of his jarred harmony, —

If here he venture to unroll
His index of adagios,
And he be given to console
Humanity with what he knows, —

He may by contemplation learn
A little more than what he knew,
And even see great oaks return
To acorns out of which they grew.

He may, if he but listen well,
Through twilight and the silence here,

Be told what there are none may tell
To vanity's impatient ear;

And he may never dare again
Say what awaits him, or be sure
What sunlit labyrinth of pain
He may not enter and endure.

Who knows to-day from yesterday
May learn to count no thing too strange:
Love builds of what Time takes away,
Till Death itself is less than Change.

Who sees enough in his duress
May go as far as dreams have gone;
Who sees a little may do less
Than many who are blind have done;

Who sees unchastened here the soul
Triumphant has no other sight
Than has a child who sees the whole
World radiant with his own delight.

Far journeys and hard wandering
Await him in whose crude surmise
Peace, like a mask, hides everything
That is and has been from his eyes;

And all his wisdom is unfound,
Or like a web that error weaves
On airy looms that have a sound
No louder now than falling leaves.

Old King Cole

In Tilbury Town did Old King Cole
A wise old age anticipate,
Desiring, with his pipe and bowl,
No Khan's extravagant estate.
No crown annoyed his honest head,
No fiddlers three were called or needed;
For two disastrous heirs instead
Made music more than ever three did.

Bereft of her with whom his life
Was harmony without a flaw,
He took no other for a wife,
Nor sighed for any that he saw;
And if he doubted his two sons,
And heirs, Alexis and Evander,
He might have been as doubtful once
Of Robert Burns and Alexander.

Alexis, in his early youth,
Began to steal — from old and young.
Likewise Evander, and the truth
Was like a bad taste on his tongue.
Born thieves and liars, their affair
Seemed only to be tarred with evil —
The most insufferable pair
Of scamps that ever cheered the devil.

The world went on, their fame went on,
And they went on — from bad to worse;
Till, goaded hot with nothing done,
And each accoutred with a curse,
The friends of Old King Cole, by twos,
And fours, and sevens, and elevens,
Pronounced unalterable views

Of doings that were not of heaven's.

And having learned again whereby
Their baleful zeal had come about,
King Cole met many a wrathful eye
So kindly that its wrath went out —
Or partly out. Say what they would,
He seemed the more to court their candor;
But never told what kind of good
Was in Alexis and Evander.

And Old King Cole, with many a puff
That haloed his urbanity,
Would smoke till he had smoked enough,
And listen most attentively.
He beamed as with an inward light
That had the Lord's assurance in it;
And once a man was there all night,
Expecting something every minute.

But whether from too little thought,
Or too much fealty to the bowl,
A dim reward was all he got
For sitting up with Old King Cole.
"Though mine," the father mused aloud,
"Are not the sons I would have chosen,
Shall I, less evilly endowed,
By their infirmity be frozen?

"They'll have a bad end, I'll agree,
But I was never born to groan;
For I can see what I can see,
And I'm accordingly alone.
With open heart and open door,
I love my friends, I like my neighbors;
But if I try to tell you more,
Your doubts will overmatch my labors.

"This pipe would never make me calm,
This bowl my grief would never drown.

For grief like mine there is no balm
In Gilead, or in Tilbury Town.
And if I see what I can see,
I know not any way to blind it;
Nor more if any way may be
For you to grope or fly to find it.

"There may be room for ruin yet,
And ashes for a wasted love;
Or, like One whom you may forget,
I may have meat you know not of.
And if I'd rather live than weep
Meanwhile, do you find that surprising?
Why, bless my soul, the man's asleep!
That's good. The sun will soon be rising."

Ben Jonson Entertains a Man from Stratford

You are a friend then, as I make it out,
Of our man Shakespeare, who alone of us
Will put an ass's head in Fairyland
As he would add a shilling to more shillings,
All most harmonious, — and out of his
Miraculous inviolable increase
Fills Ilion, Rome, or any town you like
Of olden time with timeless Englishmen;
And I must wonder what you think of him —
All you down there where your small Avon flows
By Stratford, and where you're an Alderman.
Some, for a guess, would have him riding back
To be a farrier there, or say a dyer;
Or maybe one of your adept surveyors;
Or like enough the wizard of all tanners.
Not you — no fear of that; for I discern
In you a kindling of the flame that saves —
The nimble element, the true phlogiston;
I see it, and was told of it, moreover,
By our discriminate friend himself, no other.
Had you been one of the sad average,
As he would have it, — meaning, as I take it,
The sinew and the solvent of our Island,
You'd not be buying beer for this Terpander's
Approved and estimated friend Ben Jonson;
He'd never foist it as a part of his
Contingent entertainment of a townsman
While he goes off rehearsing, as he must,
If he shall ever be the Duke of Stratford.
And my words are no shadow on your town —
Far from it; for one town's as like another
As all are unlike London. Oh, he knows it, —
And there's the Stratford in him; he denies it,
And there's the Shakespeare in him. So, God help him!

I tell him he needs Greek; but neither God
Nor Greek will help him. Nothing will help that man.
You see the fates have given him so much,
He must have all or perish, — or look out
Of London, where he sees too many lords;
They're part of half what ails him: I suppose
There's nothing fouler down among the demons
Than what it is he feels when he remembers
The dust and sweat and ointment of his calling
With his lords looking on and laughing at him.
King as he is, he can't be king ~de facto~,
And that's as well, because he wouldn't like it;
He'd frame a lower rating of men then
Than he has now; and after that would come
An abdication or an apoplexy.
He can't be king, not even king of Stratford, —
Though half the world, if not the whole of it,
May crown him with a crown that fits no king
Save Lord Apollo's homesick emissary:
Not there on Avon, or on any stream
Where Naiads and their white arms are no more,
Shall he find home again. It's all too bad.
But there's a comfort, for he'll have that House —
The best you ever saw; and he'll be there
Anon, as you're an Alderman. Good God!
He makes me lie awake o' nights and laugh.
And you have known him from his origin,
You tell me; and a most uncommon urchin
He must have been to the few seeing ones —
A trifle terrifying, I dare say,
Discovering a world with his man's eyes,
Quite as another lad might see some finches,
If he looked hard and had an eye for nature.
But this one had his eyes and their foretelling,
And he had you to fare with, and what else?
He must have had a father and a mother —
In fact I've heard him say so — and a dog,
As a boy should, I venture; and the dog,
Most likely, was the only man who knew him.
A dog, for all I know, is what he needs

As much as anything right here to-day,
To counsel him about his disillusions,
Old aches, and parturitions of what's coming, —
A dog of orders, an emeritus,
To wag his tail at him when he comes home,
And then to put his paws up on his knees
And say, "For God's sake, what's it all about?"

I don't know whether he needs a dog or not —
Or what he needs. I tell him he needs Greek;
I'll talk of rules and Aristotle with him,
And if his tongue's at home he'll say to that,
"I have your word that Aristotle knows,
And you mine that I don't know Aristotle."
He's all at odds with all the unities,
And what's yet worse, it doesn't seem to matter;
He treads along through Time's old wilderness
As if the tramp of all the centuries
Had left no roads — and there are none, for him;
He doesn't see them, even with those eyes, —
And that's a pity, or I say it is.
Accordingly we have him as we have him —
Going his way, the way that he goes best,
A pleasant animal with no great noise
Or nonsense anywhere to set him off —
Save only divers and inclement devils
Have made of late his heart their dwelling place.
A flame half ready to fly out sometimes
At some annoyance may be fanned up in him,
But soon it falls, and when it falls goes out;
He knows how little room there is in there
For crude and futile animosities,
And how much for the joy of being whole,
And how much for long sorrow and old pain.
On our side there are some who may be given
To grow old wondering what he thinks of us
And some above us, who are, in his eyes,
Above himself, — and that's quite right and English.
Yet here we smile, or disappoint the gods
Who made it so: the gods have always eyes

To see men scratch; and they see one down here
Who itches, manor-bitten to the bone,
Albeit he knows himself — yes, yes, he knows —
The lord of more than England and of more
Than all the seas of England in all time
Shall ever wash. D'ye wonder that I laugh?
He sees me, and he doesn't seem to care;
And why the devil should he? I can't tell you.

I'll meet him out alone of a bright Sunday,
Trim, rather spruce, and quite the gentleman.
"What ho, my lord!" say I. He doesn't hear me;
Wherefore I have to pause and look at him.
He's not enormous, but one looks at him.
A little on the round if you insist,
For now, God save the mark, he's growing old;
He's five and forty, and to hear him talk
These days you'd call him eighty; then you'd add
More years to that. He's old enough to be
The father of a world, and so he is.
"Ben, you're a scholar, what's the time of day?"
Says he; and there shines out of him again
An aged light that has no age or station —
The mystery that's his — a mischievous
Half-mad serenity that laughs at fame
For being won so easy, and at friends
Who laugh at him for what he wants the most,
And for his dukedom down in Warwickshire; —
By which you see we're all a little jealous. . . .
Poor Greene! I fear the color of his name
Was even as that of his ascending soul;
And he was one where there are many others, —
Some scrivening to the end against their fate,
Their puppets all in ink and all to die there;
And some with hands that once would shade an eye
That scanned Euripides and Aeschylus
Will reach by this time for a pot-house mop
To slush their first and last of royalties.
Poor devils! and they all play to his hand;
For so it was in Athens and old Rome.

But that's not here or there; I've wandered off.
Greene does it, or I'm careful. Where's that boy?

Yes, he'll go back to Stratford. And we'll miss him?
Dear sir, there'll be no London here without him.
We'll all be riding, one of these fine days,
Down there to see him — and his wife won't like us;
And then we'll think of what he never said
Of women — which, if taken all in all
With what he did say, would buy many horses.
Though nowadays he's not so much for women:
"So few of them," he says, "are worth the guessing."
But there's a work at work when he says that,
And while he says it one feels in the air
A deal of circumambient hocus-pocus.
They've had him dancing till his toes were tender,
And he can feel 'em now, come chilly rains.
There's no long cry for going into it,
However, and we don't know much about it.

The Fitton thing was worst of all, I fancy;
And you in Stratford, like most here in London,
Have more now in the ~Sonnets~ than you paid for;
He's put her there with all her poison on,
To make a singing fiction of a shadow
That's in his life a fact, and always will be.
But she's no care of ours, though Time, I fear,
Will have a more reverberant ado
About her than about another one
Who seems to have decoyed him, married him,
And sent him scuttling on his way to London, —
With much already learned, and more to learn,
And more to follow. Lord! how I see him now,
Pretending, maybe trying, to be like us.
Whatever he may have meant, we never had him;
He failed us, or escaped, or what you will, —
And there was that about him (God knows what, —
We'd flayed another had he tried it on us)
That made as many of us as had wits
More fond of all his easy distances

Than one another's noise and clap-your-shoulder.
But think you not, my friend, he'd never talk!
Talk? He was eldritch at it; and we listened —
Thereby acquiring much we knew before
About ourselves, and hitherto had held
Irrelevant, or not prime to the purpose.
And there were some, of course, and there be now,
Disordered and reduced amazedly
To resignation by the mystic seal
Of young finality the gods had laid
On everything that made him a young demon;
And one or two shot looks at him already
As he had been their executioner;
And once or twice he was, not knowing it, —
Or knowing, being sorry for poor clay
And saying nothing. . . . Yet, for all his engines,
You'll meet a thousand of an afternoon
Who strut and sun themselves and see around 'em
A world made out of more that has a reason
Than his, I swear, that he sees here to-day;
Though he may scarcely give a Fool an exit
But we mark how he sees in everything
A law that, given we flout it once too often,
Brings fire and iron down on our naked heads.
To me it looks as if the power that made him,
For fear of giving all things to one creature,
Left out the first, — faith, innocence, illusion,
Whatever 'tis that keeps us out o' Bedlam, —
And thereby, for his too consuming vision,
Empowered him out of nature; though to see him,
You'd never guess what's going on inside him.
He'll break out some day like a keg of ale
With too much independent frenzy in it;
And all for cellaring what he knows won't keep,
And what he'd best forget — but that he can't.
You'll have it, and have more than I'm foretelling;
And there'll be such a roaring at the Globe
As never stunned the bleeding gladiators.
He'll have to change the color of its hair
A bit, for now he calls it Cleopatra.

Black hair would never do for Cleopatra.

But you and I are not yet two old women,
And you're a man of office. What he does
Is more to you than how it is he does it, —
And that's what the Lord God has never told him.
They work together, and the Devil helps 'em;
They do it of a morning, or if not,
They do it of a night; in which event
He's peevish of a morning. He seems old;
He's not the proper stomach or the sleep —
And they're two sovran agents to conserve him
Against the fiery art that has no mercy
But what's in that prodigious grand new House.
I gather something happening in his boyhood
Fulfilled him with a boy's determination
To make all Stratford 'ware of him. Well, well,
I hope at last he'll have his joy of it,
And all his pigs and sheep and bellowing beeves,
And frogs and owls and unicorns, moreover,
Be less than hell to his attendant ears.
Oh, past a doubt we'll all go down to see him.

He may be wise. With London two days off,
Down there some wind of heaven may yet revive him;
But there's no quickening breath from anywhere
Shall make of him again the poised young faun
From Warwickshire, who'd made, it seems, already
A legend of himself before I came
To blink before the last of his first lightning.
Whatever there be, they'll be no more of that;
The coming on of his old monster Time
Has made him a still man; and he has dreams
Were fair to think on once, and all found hollow.
He knows how much of what men paint themselves
Would blister in the light of what they are;
He sees how much of what was great now shares
An eminence transformed and ordinary;
He knows too much of what the world has hushed
In others, to be loud now for himself;

He knows now at what height low enemies
May reach his heart, and high friends let him fall;
But what not even such as he may know
Bedevils him the worst: his lark may sing
At heaven's gate how he will, and for as long
As joy may listen; but ~he~ sees no gate,
Save one whereat the spent clay waits a little
Before the churchyard has it, and the worm.
Not long ago, late in an afternoon,
I came on him unseen down Lambeth way,
And on my life I was afear'd of him:
He gloomed and mumbled like a soul from Tophet,
His hands behind him and his head bent solemn.
"What is it now," said I, — "another woman?"
That made him sorry for me, and he smiled.
"No, Ben," he mused; "it's Nothing. It's all Nothing.
We come, we go; and when we're done, we're done;
Spiders and flies — we're mostly one or t'other —
We come, we go; and when we're done, we're done."
"By God, you sing that song as if you knew it!"
Said I, by way of cheering him; "what ails ye?"
"I think I must have come down here to think,"
Says he to that, and pulls his little beard;
"Your fly will serve as well as anybody,
And what's his hour? He flies, and flies, and flies,
And in his fly's mind has a brave appearance;
And then your spider gets him in her net,
And eats him out, and hangs him up to dry.
That's Nature, the kind mother of us all.
And then your slattern housemaid swings her broom,
And where's your spider? And that's Nature, also.
It's Nature, and it's Nothing. It's all Nothing.
It's all a world where bugs and emperors
Go singularly back to the same dust,
Each in his time; and the old, ordered stars
That sang together, Ben, will sing the same
Old stave to-morrow."

        When he talks like that,
There's nothing for a human man to do

But lead him to some grateful nook like this
Where we be now, and there to make him drink.
He'll drink, for love of me, and then be sick;
A sad sign always in a man of parts,
And always very ominous. The great
Should be as large in liquor as in love, —
And our great friend is not so large in either:
One disaffects him, and the other fails him;
Whatso he drinks that has an antic in it,
He's wondering what's to pay in his insides;
And while his eyes are on the Cyprian
He's fribbling all the time with that damned House.
We laugh here at his thrift, but after all
It may be thrift that saves him from the devil;
God gave it, anyhow, — and we'll suppose
He knew the compound of his handiwork.
To-day the clouds are with him, but anon
He'll out of 'em enough to shake the tree
Of life itself and bring down fruit unheard-of, —
And, throwing in the bruised and whole together,
Prepare a wine to make us drunk with wonder;
And if he live, there'll be a sunset spell
Thrown over him as over a glassed lake
That yesterday was all a black wild water.

God send he live to give us, if no more,
What now's a-rampage in him, and exhibit,
With a decent half-allegiance to the ages
An earnest of at least a casual eye
Turned once on what he owes to Gutenberg,
And to the fealty of more centuries
Than are as yet a picture in our vision.
"There's time enough, — I'll do it when I'm old,
And we're immortal men," he says to that;
And then he says to me, "Ben, what's 'immortal'?
Think you by any force of ordination
It may be nothing of a sort more noisy
Than a small oblivion of component ashes
That of a dream-addicted world was once
A moving atomy much like your friend here?"

Nothing will help that man. To make him laugh,
I said then he was a mad mountebank, —
And by the Lord I nearer made him cry.
I could have eat an eft then, on my knees,
Tail, claws, and all of him; for I had stung
The king of men, who had no sting for me,
And I had hurt him in his memories;
And I say now, as I shall say again,
I love the man this side idolatry.

He'll do it when he's old, he says. I wonder.
He may not be so ancient as all that.
For such as he, the thing that is to do
Will do itself, — but there's a reckoning;
The sessions that are now too much his own,
The roiling inward of a stilled outside,
The churning out of all those blood-fed lines,
The nights of many schemes and little sleep,
The full brain hammered hot with too much thinking,
The vexed heart over-worn with too much aching, —
This weary jangling of conjoined affairs
Made out of elements that have no end,
And all confused at once, I understand,
Is not what makes a man to live forever.
O no, not now! He'll not be going now:
There'll be time yet for God knows what explosions
Before he goes. He'll stay awhile. Just wait:
Just wait a year or two for Cleopatra,
For she's to be a balsam and a comfort;
And that's not all a jape of mine now, either.
For granted once the old way of Apollo
Sings in a man, he may then, if he's able,
Strike unafraid whatever strings he will
Upon the last and wildest of new lyres;
Nor out of his new magic, though it hymn
The shrieks of dungeoned hell, shall he create
A madness or a gloom to shut quite out
A cleaving daylight, and a last great calm
Triumphant over shipwreck and all storms.
He might have given Aristotle creeps,

But surely would have given him his ~katharsis~.

He'll not be going yet. There's too much yet
Unsung within the man. But when he goes,
I'd stake ye coin o' the realm his only care
For a phantom world he sounded and found wanting
Will be a portion here, a portion there,
Of this or that thing or some other thing
That has a patent and intrinsical
Equivalence in those egregious shillings.
And yet he knows, God help him! Tell me, now,
If ever there was anything let loose
On earth by gods or devils heretofore
Like this mad, careful, proud, indifferent Shakespeare!
Where was it, if it ever was? By heaven,
'Twas never yet in Rhodes or Pergamon —
In Thebes or Nineveh, a thing like this!
No thing like this was ever out of England;
And that he knows. I wonder if he cares.
Perhaps he does. . . . O Lord, that House in Stratford!

Eros Turannos

She fears him, and will always ask
 What fated her to choose him;
She meets in his engaging mask
 All reasons to refuse him;
But what she meets and what she fears
Are less than are the downward years,
Drawn slowly to the foamless weirs
 Of age, were she to lose him.

Between a blurred sagacity
 That once had power to sound him,
And Love, that will not let him be
 The Judas that she found him,
Her pride assuages her almost,
As if it were alone the cost. —
He sees that he will not be lost,
 And waits and looks around him.

A sense of ocean and old trees
 Envelops and allures him;
Tradition, touching all he sees,
 Beguiles and reassures him;
And all her doubts of what he says
Are dimmed of what she knows of days —
Till even prejudice delays
 And fades, and she secures him.

The falling leaf inaugurates
 The reign of her confusion;
The pounding wave reverberates
 The dirge of her illusion;
And home, where passion lived and died,
Becomes a place where she can hide,
While all the town and harbor side

Vibrate with her seclusion.

We tell you, tapping on our brows,
 The story as it should be, —
As if the story of a house
 Were told, or ever could be;
We'll have no kindly veil between
Her visions and those we have seen, —
As if we guessed what hers have been,
 Or what they are or would be.

Meanwhile we do no harm; for they
 That with a god have striven,
Not hearing much of what we say,
 Take what the god has given;
Though like waves breaking it may be,
Or like a changed familiar tree,
Or like a stairway to the sea
 Where down the blind are driven.
Old Trails

Washington Square

I met him, as one meets a ghost or two,
Between the gray Arch and the old Hotel.
"King Solomon was right, there's nothing new,"
Said he. "Behold a ruin who meant well."

He led me down familiar steps again,
Appealingly, and set me in a chair.
"My dreams have all come true to other men,"
Said he; "God lives, however, and why care?

"An hour among the ghosts will do no harm."
He laughed, and something glad within me sank.
I may have eyed him with a faint alarm,
For now his laugh was lost in what he drank.

"They chill things here with ice from hell," he said;
"I might have known it." And he made a face
That showed again how much of him was dead,
And how much was alive and out of place,

And out of reach. He knew as well as I
That all the words of wise men who are skilled
In using them are not much to defy
What comes when memory meets the unfulfilled.

What evil and infirm perversity
Had been at work with him to bring him back?
Never among the ghosts, assuredly,
Would he originate a new attack;

Never among the ghosts, or anywhere,
Till what was dead of him was put away,
Would he attain to his offended share
Of honor among others of his day.

"You ponder like an owl," he said at last;
"You always did, and here you have a cause.
For I'm a confirmation of the past,
A vengeance, and a flowering of what was.

"Sorry? Of course you are, though you compress,
With even your most impenetrable fears,
A placid and a proper consciousness
Of anxious angels over my arrears.

"I see them there against me in a book
As large as hope, in ink that shines by night.
For sure I see; but now I'd rather look
At you, and you are not a pleasant sight.

"Forbear, forgive. Ten years are on my soul,
And on my conscience. I've an incubus:
My one distinction, and a parlous toll
To glory; but hope lives on clamorous.

"'Twas hope, though heaven I grant you knows of what —
The kind that blinks and rises when it falls,
Whether it sees a reason why or not —
That heard Broadway's hard-throated siren-calls;

"'Twas hope that brought me through December storms,
To shores again where I'll not have to be
A lonely man with only foreign worms
To cheer him in his last obscurity.

"But what it was that hurried me down here
To be among the ghosts, I leave to you.
My thanks are yours, no less, for one thing clear:
Though you are silent, what you say is true.

"There may have been the devil in my feet,
For down I blundered, like a fugitive,
To find the old room in Eleventh Street.
God save us! — I came here again to live."

We rose at that, and all the ghosts rose then,
And followed us unseen to his old room.
No longer a good place for living men
We found it, and we shivered in the gloom.

The goods he took away from there were few,
And soon we found ourselves outside once more,
Where now the lamps along the Avenue
Bloomed white for miles above an iron floor.

"Now lead me to the newest of hotels,"
He said, "and let your spleen be undeceived:
This ruin is not myself, but some one else;
I haven't failed; I've merely not achieved."

Whether he knew or not, he laughed and dined
With more of an immune regardlessness
Of pits before him and of sands behind
Than many a child at forty would confess;

And after, when the bells in *Boris* rang
Their tumult at the Metropolitan,
He rocked himself, and I believe he sang.
"God lives," he crooned aloud, "and I'm the man!"

He was. And even though the creature spoiled
All prophecies, I cherish his acclaim.
Three weeks he fattened; and five years he toiled
In Yonkers, — and then sauntered into fame.

And he may go now to what streets he will —
Eleventh, or the last, and little care;
But he would find the old room very still
Of evenings, and the ghosts would all be there.

I doubt if he goes after them; I doubt
If many of them ever come to him.
His memories are like lamps, and they go out;
Or if they burn, they flicker and are dim.

A light of other gleams he has to-day
And adulations of applauding hosts;
A famous danger, but a safer way
Than growing old alone among the ghosts.

But we may still be glad that we were wrong:
He fooled us, and we'd shrivel to deny it;
Though sometimes when old echoes ring too long,
I wish the bells in *Boris* would be quiet.

The Unforgiven

When he, who is the unforgiven,
Beheld her first, he found her fair:
No promise ever dreamt in heaven
Could then have lured him anywhere
That would have been away from there;
And all his wits had lightly striven,
Foiled with her voice, and eyes, and hair.

There's nothing in the saints and sages
To meet the shafts her glances had,
Or such as hers have had for ages
To blind a man till he be glad,
And humble him till he be mad.
The story would have many pages,
And would be neither good nor bad.

And, having followed, you would find him
Where properly the play begins;
But look for no red light behind him —
No fumes of many-colored sins,
Fanned high by screaming violins.
God knows what good it was to blind him,
Or whether man or woman wins.

And by the same eternal token,
Who knows just how it will all end? —
This drama of hard words unspoken,
This fireside farce, without a friend
Or enemy to comprehend
What augurs when two lives are broken,
And fear finds nothing left to mend.

He stares in vain for what awaits him,
And sees in Love a coin to toss;

He smiles, and her cold hush berates him
Beneath his hard half of the cross;
They wonder why it ever was;
And she, the unforgiving, hates him
More for her lack than for her loss.

He feeds with pride his indecision,
And shrinks from what will not occur,
Bequeathing with infirm derision
His ashes to the days that were,
Before she made him prisoner;
And labors to retrieve the vision
That he must once have had of her.

He waits, and there awaits an ending,
And he knows neither what nor when;
But no magicians are attending
To make him see as he saw then,
And he will never find again
The face that once had been the rending
Of all his purpose among men.

He blames her not, nor does he chide her,
And she has nothing new to say;
If he were Bluebeard he could hide her,
But that's not written in the play,
And there will be no change to-day;
Although, to the serene outsider,
There still would seem to be a way.

Theophilus

By what serene malevolence of names
Had you the gift of yours, Theophilus?
Not even a smeared young Cyclops at his games
Would have you long, — and you are one of us.

Told of your deeds I shudder for your dreams,
And they, no doubt, are few and innocent.
Meanwhile, I marvel; for in you, it seems,
Heredity outshines environment.

What lingering bit of Belial, unforeseen,
Survives and amplifies itself in you?
What manner of devilry has ever been
That your obliquity may never do?

Humility befits a father's eyes,
But not a friend of us would have him weep.
Admiring everything that lives and dies,
Theophilus, we like you best asleep.

Sleep — sleep; and let us find another man
To lend another name less hazardous:
Caligula, maybe, or Caliban,
Or Cain, — but surely not Theophilus.

Veteran Sirens

The ghost of Ninon would be sorry now
To laugh at them, were she to see them here,
So brave and so alert for learning how
To fence with reason for another year.

Age offers a far comelier diadem
Than theirs; but anguish has no eye for grace,
When time's malicious mercy cautions them
To think a while of number and of space.

The burning hope, the worn expectancy,
The martyred humor, and the maimed allure,
Cry out for time to end his levity,
And age to soften its investiture;

But they, though others fade and are still fair,
Defy their fairness and are unsubdued;
Although they suffer, they may not forswear
The patient ardor of the unpursued.

Poor flesh, to fight the calendar so long;
Poor vanity, so quaint and yet so brave;
Poor folly, so deceived and yet so strong,
So far from Ninon and so near the grave.

Siege Perilous

Long warned of many terrors more severe
To scorch him than hell's engines could awaken,
He scanned again, too far to be so near,
The fearful seat no man had ever taken.

So many other men with older eyes
Than his to see with older sight behind them
Had known so long their one way to be wise, —
Was any other thing to do than mind them?

So many a blasting parallel had seared
Confusion on his faith, — could he but wonder
If he were mad and right, or if he feared
God's fury told in shafted flame and thunder?

There fell one day upon his eyes a light
Ethereal, and he heard no more men speaking;
He saw their shaken heads, but no long sight
Was his but for the end that he went seeking.

The end he sought was not the end; the crown
He won shall unto many still be given.
Moreover, there was reason here to frown:
No fury thundered, no flame fell from heaven.

Another Dark Lady

Think not, because I wonder where you fled,
That I would lift a pin to see you there;
You may, for me, be prowling anywhere,
So long as you show not your little head:
No dark and evil story of the dead
Would leave you less pernicious or less fair —
Not even Lilith, with her famous hair;
And Lilith was the devil, I have read.
I cannot hate you, for I loved you then.
The woods were golden then. There was a road
Through beeches; and I said their smooth feet showed
Like yours. Truth must have heard me from afar,
For I shall never have to learn again
That yours are cloven as no beech's are.

The Voice of Age

She'd look upon us, if she could,
As hard as Rhadamanthus would;
Yet one may see, — who sees her face,
Her crown of silver and of lace,
Her mystical serene address
Of age alloyed with loveliness, —
That she would not annihilate
The frailest of things animate.

She has opinions of our ways,
And if we're not all mad, she says, —
If our ways are not wholly worse
Than others, for not being hers, —
There might somehow be found a few
Less insane things for us to do,
And we might have a little heed
Of what Belshazzar couldn't read.

She feels, with all our furniture,
Room yet for something more secure
Than our self-kindled aureoles
To guide our poor forgotten souls;
But when we have explained that grace
Dwells now in doing for the race,
She nods — as if she were relieved;
Almost as if she were deceived.

She frowns at much of what she hears,
And shakes her head, and has her fears;
Though none may know, by any chance,
What rose-leaf ashes of romance
Are faintly stirred by later days
That would be well enough, she says,
If only people were more wise,
And grown-up children used their eyes.

The Dark House

Where a faint light shines alone,
Dwells a Demon I have known.
Most of you had better say
"The Dark House", and go your way.
Do not wonder if I stay.

For I know the Demon's eyes,
And their lure that never dies.
Banish all your fond alarms,
For I know the foiling charms
Of her eyes and of her arms,

And I know that in one room
Burns a lamp as in a tomb;
And I see the shadow glide,
Back and forth, of one denied
Power to find himself outside.

There he is who is my friend,
Damned, he fancies, to the end —
Vanquished, ever since a door
Closed, he thought, for evermore
On the life that was before.

And the friend who knows him best
Sees him as he sees the rest
Who are striving to be wise
While a Demon's arms and eyes
Hold them as a web would flies.

All the words of all the world,
Aimed together and then hurled,
Would be stiller in his ears
Than a closing of still shears
On a thread made out of years.

But there lives another sound,
More compelling, more profound;
There's a music, so it seems,
That assuages and redeems,
More than reason, more than dreams.

There's a music yet unheard
By the creature of the word,
Though it matters little more
Than a wave-wash on a shore —
Till a Demon shuts a door.

So, if he be very still
With his Demon, and one will,
Murmurs of it may be blown
To my friend who is alone
In a room that I have known.

After that from everywhere
Singing life will find him there;
Then the door will open wide,
And my friend, again outside,
Will be living, having died.

The Poor Relation

No longer torn by what she knows
And sees within the eyes of others,
Her doubts are when the daylight goes,
Her fears are for the few she bothers.
She tells them it is wholly wrong
Of her to stay alive so long;
And when she smiles her forehead shows
A crinkle that had been her mother's.

Beneath her beauty, blanched with pain,
And wistful yet for being cheated,
A child would seem to ask again
A question many times repeated;
But no rebellion has betrayed
Her wonder at what she has paid
For memories that have no stain,
For triumph born to be defeated.

To those who come for what she was —
The few left who know where to find her —
She clings, for they are all she has;
And she may smile when they remind her,
As heretofore, of what they know
Of roses that are still to blow
By ways where not so much as grass
Remains of what she sees behind her.

They stay a while, and having done
What penance or the past requires,
They go, and leave her there alone
To count her chimneys and her spires.
Her lip shakes when they go away,
And yet she would not have them stay;
She knows as well as anyone
That Pity, having played, soon tires.

But one friend always reappears,
A good ghost, not to be forsaken;
Whereat she laughs and has no fears
Of what a ghost may reawaken,
But welcomes, while she wears and mends
The poor relation's odds and ends,
Her truant from a tomb of years —
Her power of youth so early taken.

Poor laugh, more slender than her song
It seems; and there are none to hear it
With even the stopped ears of the strong
For breaking heart or broken spirit.
The friends who clamored for her place,
And would have scratched her for her face,
Have lost her laughter for so long
That none would care enough to fear it.

None live who need fear anything
From her, whose losses are their pleasure;
The plover with a wounded wing
Stays not the flight that others measure;
So there she waits, and while she lives,
And death forgets, and faith forgives,
Her memories go foraging
For bits of childhood song they treasure.

And like a giant harp that hums
On always, and is always blending
The coming of what never comes
With what has past and had an ending,
The City trembles, throbs, and pounds
Outside, and through a thousand sounds
The small intolerable drums
Of Time are like slow drops descending.

Bereft enough to shame a sage
And given little to long sighing,
With no illusion to assuage

The lonely changelessness of dying, —
Unsought, unthought-of, and unheard,
She sings and watches like a bird,
Safe in a comfortable cage
From which there will be no more flying.
The Burning Book

Or the Contented Metaphysician

To the lore of no manner of men
 Would his vision have yielded
When he found what will never again
 From his vision be shielded, —
Though he paid with as much of his life
 As a nun could have given,
And to-night would have been as a knife,
 Devil-drawn, devil-driven.

For to-night, with his flame-weary eyes
 On the work he is doing,
He considers the tinder that flies
 And the quick flame pursuing.
In the leaves that are crinkled and curled
 Are his ashes of glory,
And what once were an end of the world
 Is an end of a story.

But he smiles, for no more shall his days
 Be a toil and a calling
For a way to make others to gaze
 On God's face without falling.
He has come to the end of his words,
 And alone he rejoices
In the choiring that silence affords
 Of ineffable voices.

To a realm that his words may not reach
 He may lead none to find him;
An adept, and with nothing to teach,
 He leaves nothing behind him.
For the rest, he will have his release,
 And his embers, attended
By the large and unclamoring peace
 Of a dream that is ended.

Fragment

Faint white pillars that seem to fade
As you look from here are the first one sees
Of his house where it hides and dies in a shade
Of beeches and oaks and hickory trees.
Now many a man, given woods like these,
And a house like that, and the Briony gold,
Would have said, "There are still some gods to please,
And houses are built without hands, we're told."

There are the pillars, and all gone gray.
Briony's hair went white. You may see
Where the garden was if you come this way.
That sun-dial scared him, he said to me;
"Sooner or later they strike," said he,
And he never got that from the books he read.
Others are flourishing, worse than he,
But he knew too much for the life he led.

And who knows all knows everything
That a patient ghost at last retrieves;
There's more to be known of his harvesting
When Time the thresher unbinds the sheaves;
And there's more to be heard than a wind that grieves
For Briony now in this ageless oak,
Driving the first of its withered leaves
Over the stones where the fountain broke.
Lisette and Eileen

"When he was here alive, Eileen,
There was a word you might have said;
So never mind what I have been,
Or anything, — for you are dead.

"And after this when I am there
Where he is, you'll be dying still.
Your eyes are dead, and your black hair, —
The rest of you be what it will.

"'Twas all to save him? Never mind,
Eileen. You saved him. You are strong.
I'd hardly wonder if your kind
Paid everything, for you live long.

"You last, I mean. That's what I mean.
I mean you last as long as lies.
You might have said that word, Eileen, —
And you might have your hair and eyes.

"And what you see might be Lisette,
Instead of this that has no name.
Your silence — I can feel it yet,
Alive and in me, like a flame.

"Where might I be with him to-day,
Could he have known before he heard?
But no — your silence had its way,
Without a weapon or a word.

"Because a word was never told,
I'm going as a worn toy goes.
And you are dead; and you'll be old;
And I forgive you, I suppose.

"I'll soon be changing as all do,
To something we have always been;
And you'll be old . . . He liked you, too.
I might have killed you then, Eileen,

"I think he liked as much of you
As had a reason to be seen, —
As much as God made black and blue.
He liked your hair and eyes, Eileen."

Llewellyn and the Tree

Could he have made Priscilla share
 The paradise that he had planned,
Llewellyn would have loved his wife
 As well as any in the land.

Could he have made Priscilla cease
 To goad him for what God left out,
Llewellyn would have been as mild
 As any we have read about.

Could all have been as all was not,
 Llewellyn would have had no story;
He would have stayed a quiet man
 And gone his quiet way to glory.

But howsoever mild he was
 Priscilla was implacable;
And whatsoever timid hopes
 He built — she found them, and they fell.

And this went on, with intervals
 Of labored harmony between
Resounding discords, till at last
 Llewellyn turned — as will be seen.

Priscilla, warmer than her name,
 And shriller than the sound of saws,
Pursued Llewellyn once too far,
 Not knowing quite the man he was.

The more she said, the fiercer clung
 The stinging garment of his wrath;
And this was all before the day
 When Time tossed roses in his path.

Before the roses ever came
 Llewellyn had already risen.
The roses may have ruined him,
 They may have kept him out of prison.

And she who brought them, being Fate,
 Made roses do the work of spears, —
Though many made no more of her
 Than civet, coral, rouge, and years.

You ask us what Llewellyn saw,
 But why ask what may not be given?
To some will come a time when change
 Itself is beauty, if not heaven.

One afternoon Priscilla spoke,
 And her shrill history was done;
At any rate, she never spoke
 Like that again to anyone.

One gold October afternoon
 Great fury smote the silent air;
And then Llewellyn leapt and fled
 Like one with hornets in his hair.

Llewellyn left us, and he said
 Forever, leaving few to doubt him;
And so, through frost and clicking leaves,
 The Tilbury way went on without him.

And slowly, through the Tilbury mist,
 The stillness of October gold
Went out like beauty from a face,
 Priscilla watched it, and grew old.

He fled, still clutching in his flight
 The roses that had been his fall;
The Scarlet One, as you surmise,
 Fled with him, coral, rouge, and all.

Priscilla, waiting, saw the change
　Of twenty slow October moons;
And then she vanished, in her turn
　To be forgotten, like old tunes.

So they were gone — all three of them,
　I should have said, and said no more,
Had not a face once on Broadway
　Been one that I had seen before.

The face and hands and hair were old,
　But neither time nor penury
Could quench within Llewellyn's eyes
　The shine of his one victory.

The roses, faded and gone by,
　Left ruin where they once had reigned;
But on the wreck, as on old shells,
　The color of the rose remained.

His fictive merchandise I bought
　For him to keep and show again,
Then led him slowly from the crush
　Of his cold-shouldered fellow men.

"And so, Llewellyn," I began —
　"Not so," he said; "not so, at all:
I've tried the world, and found it good,
　For more than twenty years this fall.

"And what the world has left of me
　Will go now in a little while."
And what the world had left of him
　Was partly an unholy guile.

"That I have paid for being calm
　Is what you see, if you have eyes;
For let a man be calm too long,
　He pays for much before he dies.

"Be calm when you are growing old
  And you have nothing else to do;
Pour not the wine of life too thin
  If water means the death of you.

"You say I might have learned at home
  The truth in season to be strong?
Not so; I took the wine of life
  Too thin, and I was calm too long.

"Like others who are strong too late,
  For me there was no going back;
For I had found another speed,
  And I was on the other track.

"God knows how far I might have gone
  Or what there might have been to see;
But my speed had a sudden end,
  And here you have the end of me."

The end or not, it may be now
  But little farther from the truth
To say those worn satiric eyes
  Had something of immortal youth.

He may among the millions here
  Be one; or he may, quite as well,
Be gone to find again the Tree
  Of Knowledge, out of which he fell.

He may be near us, dreaming yet
  Of unrepented rouge and coral;
Or in a grave without a name
  May be as far off as a moral.

Bewick Finzer

Time was when his half million drew
 The breath of six per cent;
But soon the worm of what-was-not
 Fed hard on his content;
And something crumbled in his brain
 When his half million went.

Time passed, and filled along with his
 The place of many more;
Time came, and hardly one of us
 Had credence to restore,
From what appeared one day, the man
 Whom we had known before.

The broken voice, the withered neck,
 The coat worn out with care,
The cleanliness of indigence,
 The brilliance of despair,
The fond imponderable dreams
 Of affluence, — all were there.

Poor Finzer, with his dreams and schemes,
 Fares hard now in the race,
With heart and eye that have a task
 When he looks in the face
Of one who might so easily
 Have been in Finzer's place.

He comes unfailing for the loan
 We give and then forget;
He comes, and probably for years
 Will he be coming yet, —
Familiar as an old mistake,
 And futile as regret.

Bokardo

Well, Bokardo, here we are;
 Make yourself at home.
Look around — you haven't far
 To look — and why be dumb?
Not the place that used to be,
Not so many things to see;
But there's room for you and me.
 And you — you've come.

Talk a little; or, if not,
 Show me with a sign
Why it was that you forgot
 What was yours and mine.
Friends, I gather, are small things
In an age when coins are kings;
Even at that, one hardly flings
 Friends before swine.

Rather strong? I knew as much,
 For it made you speak.
No offense to swine, as such,
 But why this hide-and-seek?
You have something on your side,
And you wish you might have died,
So you tell me. And you tried
 One night last week?

You tried hard? And even then
 Found a time to pause?
When you try as hard again,
 You'll have another cause.
When you find yourself at odds
With all dreamers of all gods,
You may smite yourself with rods —

But not the laws.

Though they seem to show a spite
 Rather devilish,
They move on as with a might
 Stronger than your wish.
Still, however strong they be,
They bide man's authority:
Xerxes, when he flogged the sea,
 May've scared a fish.

It's a comfort, if you like,
 To keep honor warm,
But as often as you strike
 The laws, you do no harm.
To the laws, I mean. To you —
That's another point of view,
One you may as well indue
 With some alarm.

Not the most heroic face
 To present, I grant;
Nor will you insure disgrace
 By fearing what you want.
Freedom has a world of sides,
And if reason once derides
Courage, then your courage hides
 A deal of cant.

Learn a little to forget
 Life was once a feast;
You aren't fit for dying yet,
 So don't be a beast.
Few men with a mind will say,
Thinking twice, that they can pay
Half their debts of yesterday,
 Or be released.

There's a debt now on your mind
 More than any gold?

And there's nothing you can find
  Out there in the cold?
Only — what's his name? — Remorse?
And Death riding on his horse?
Well, be glad there's nothing worse
  Than you have told.

Leave Remorse to warm his hands
  Outside in the rain.
As for Death, he understands,
  And he will come again.
Therefore, till your wits are clear,
Flourish and be quiet — here.
But a devil at each ear
  Will be a strain?

Past a doubt they will indeed,
  More than you have earned.
I say that because you need
  Ablution, being burned?
Well, if you must have it so,
Your last flight went rather low.
Better say you had to know
  What you have learned.

And that's over. Here you are,
  Battered by the past.
Time will have his little scar,
  But the wound won't last.
Nor shall harrowing surprise
Find a world without its eyes
If a star fades when the skies
  Are overcast.

God knows there are lives enough,
  Crushed, and too far gone
Longer to make sermons of,
  And those we leave alone.
Others, if they will, may rend
The worn patience of a friend

Who, though smiling, sees the end,
 With nothing done.

But your fervor to be free
 Fled the faith it scorned;
Death demands a decency
 Of you, and you are warned.
But for all we give we get
Mostly blows? Don't be upset;
You, Bokardo, are not yet
 Consumed or mourned.

There'll be falling into view
 Much to rearrange;
And there'll be a time for you
 To marvel at the change.
They that have the least to fear
Question hardest what is here;
When long-hidden skies are clear,
 The stars look strange.
The Man against the Sky

Between me and the sunset, like a dome
Against the glory of a world on fire,
Now burned a sudden hill,
Bleak, round, and high, by flame-lit height made higher,
With nothing on it for the flame to kill
Save one who moved and was alone up there
To loom before the chaos and the glare
As if he were the last god going home
Unto his last desire.
Dark, marvelous, and inscrutable he moved on
Till down the fiery distance he was gone, —
Like one of those eternal, remote things
That range across a man's imaginings
When a sure music fills him and he knows
What he may say thereafter to few men, —
The touch of ages having wrought
An echo and a glimpse of what he thought
A phantom or a legend until then;

For whether lighted over ways that save,
Or lured from all repose,
If he go on too far to find a grave,
Mostly alone he goes.

Even he, who stood where I had found him,
On high with fire all round him, —
Who moved along the molten west,
And over the round hill's crest
That seemed half ready with him to go down,
Flame-bitten and flame-cleft, —
As if there were to be no last thing left
Of a nameless unimaginable town, —
Even he who climbed and vanished may have taken
Down to the perils of a depth not known,
From death defended though by men forsaken,
The bread that every man must eat alone;
He may have walked while others hardly dared
Look on to see him stand where many fell;
And upward out of that, as out of hell,
He may have sung and striven
To mount where more of him shall yet be given,
Bereft of all retreat,
To sevenfold heat, —
As on a day when three in Dura shared
The furnace, and were spared
For glory by that king of Babylon
Who made himself so great that God, who heard,
Covered him with long feathers, like a bird.

Again, he may have gone down easily,
By comfortable altitudes, and found,
As always, underneath him solid ground
Whereon to be sufficient and to stand
Possessed already of the promised land,
Far stretched and fair to see:
A good sight, verily,
And one to make the eyes of her who bore him
Shine glad with hidden tears.
Why question of his ease of who before him,

In one place or another where they left
Their names as far behind them as their bones,
And yet by dint of slaughter toil and theft,
And shrewdly sharpened stones,
Carved hard the way for his ascendency
Through deserts of lost years?
Why trouble him now who sees and hears
No more than what his innocence requires,
And therefore to no other height aspires
Than one at which he neither quails nor tires?
He may do more by seeing what he sees
Than others eager for iniquities;
He may, by seeing all things for the best,
Incite futurity to do the rest.

Or with an even likelihood,
He may have met with atrabilious eyes
The fires of time on equal terms and passed
Indifferently down, until at last
His only kind of grandeur would have been,
Apparently, in being seen.
He may have had for evil or for good
No argument; he may have had no care
For what without himself went anywhere
To failure or to glory, and least of all
For such a stale, flamboyant miracle;
He may have been the prophet of an art
Immovable to old idolatries;
He may have been a player without a part,
Annoyed that even the sun should have the skies
For such a flaming way to advertise;
He may have been a painter sick at heart
With Nature's toiling for a new surprise;
He may have been a cynic, who now, for all
Of anything divine that his effete
Negation may have tasted,
Saw truth in his own image, rather small,
Forbore to fever the ephemeral,
Found any barren height a good retreat
From any swarming street,

And in the sun saw power superbly wasted;
And when the primitive old-fashioned stars
Came out again to shine on joys and wars
More primitive, and all arrayed for doom,
He may have proved a world a sorry thing
In his imagining,
And life a lighted highway to the tomb.

Or, mounting with infirm unsearching tread,
His hopes to chaos led,
He may have stumbled up there from the past,
And with an aching strangeness viewed the last
Abysmal conflagration of his dreams, —
A flame where nothing seems
To burn but flame itself, by nothing fed;
And while it all went out,
Not even the faint anodyne of doubt
May then have eased a painful going down
From pictured heights of power and lost renown,
Revealed at length to his outlived endeavor
Remote and unapproachable forever;
And at his heart there may have gnawed
Sick memories of a dead faith foiled and flawed
And long dishonored by the living death
Assigned alike by chance
To brutes and hierophants;
And anguish fallen on those he loved around him
May once have dealt the last blow to confound him,
And so have left him as death leaves a child,
Who sees it all too near;
And he who knows no young way to forget
May struggle to the tomb unreconciled.
Whatever suns may rise or set
There may be nothing kinder for him here
Than shafts and agonies;
And under these
He may cry out and stay on horribly;
Or, seeing in death too small a thing to fear,
He may go forward like a stoic Roman
Where pangs and terrors in his pathway lie, —

Or, seizing the swift logic of a woman,
Curse God and die.

Or maybe there, like many another one
Who might have stood aloft and looked ahead,
Black-drawn against wild red,
He may have built, unawed by fiery gules
That in him no commotion stirred,
A living reason out of molecules
Why molecules occurred,
And one for smiling when he might have sighed
Had he seen far enough,
And in the same inevitable stuff
Discovered an odd reason too for pride
In being what he must have been by laws
Infrangible and for no kind of cause.
Deterred by no confusion or surprise
He may have seen with his mechanic eyes
A world without a meaning, and had room,
Alone amid magnificence and doom,
To build himself an airy monument
That should, or fail him in his vague intent,
Outlast an accidental universe —
To call it nothing worse —
Or, by the burrowing guile
Of Time disintegrated and effaced,
Like once-remembered mighty trees go down
To ruin, of which by man may now be traced
No part sufficient even to be rotten,
And in the book of things that are forgotten
Is entered as a thing not quite worth while.
He may have been so great
That satraps would have shivered at his frown,
And all he prized alive may rule a state
No larger than a grave that holds a clown;
He may have been a master of his fate,
And of his atoms, — ready as another
In his emergence to exonerate
His father and his mother;
He may have been a captain of a host,

Self-eloquent and ripe for prodigies,
Doomed here to swell by dangerous degrees,
And then give up the ghost.
Nahum's great grasshoppers were such as these,
Sun-scattered and soon lost.

Whatever the dark road he may have taken,
This man who stood on high
And faced alone the sky,
Whatever drove or lured or guided him, —
A vision answering a faith unshaken,
An easy trust assumed of easy trials,
A sick negation born of weak denials,
A crazed abhorrence of an old condition,
A blind attendance on a brief ambition, —
Whatever stayed him or derided him,
His way was even as ours;
And we, with all our wounds and all our powers,
Must each await alone at his own height
Another darkness or another light;
And there, of our poor self dominion reft,
If inference and reason shun
Hell, Heaven, and Oblivion,
May thwarted will (perforce precarious,
But for our conservation better thus)
Have no misgiving left
Of doing yet what here we leave undone?
Or if unto the last of these we cleave,
Believing or protesting we believe
In such an idle and ephemeral
Florescence of the diabolical, —
If, robbed of two fond old enormities,
Our being had no onward auguries,
What then were this great love of ours to say
For launching other lives to voyage again
A little farther into time and pain,
A little faster in a futile chase
For a kingdom and a power and a Race
That would have still in sight
A manifest end of ashes and eternal night?

Is this the music of the toys we shake
So loud, — as if there might be no mistake
Somewhere in our indomitable will?
Are we no greater than the noise we make
Along one blind atomic pilgrimage
Whereon by crass chance billeted we go
Because our brains and bones and cartilage
Will have it so?
If this we say, then let us all be still
About our share in it, and live and die
More quietly thereby.

Where was he going, this man against the sky?
You know not, nor do I.
But this we know, if we know anything:
That we may laugh and fight and sing
And of our transience here make offering
To an orient Word that will not be erased,
Or, save in incommunicable gleams
Too permanent for dreams,
Be found or known.
No tonic and ambitious irritant
Of increase or of want
Has made an otherwise insensate waste
Of ages overthrown
A ruthless, veiled, implacable foretaste
Of other ages that are still to be
Depleted and rewarded variously
Because a few, by fate's economy,
Shall seem to move the world the way it goes;
No soft evangel of equality,
Safe cradled in a communal repose
That huddles into death and may at last
Be covered well with equatorial snows —
And all for what, the devil only knows —
Will aggregate an inkling to confirm
The credit of a sage or of a worm,
Or tell us why one man in five
Should have a care to stay alive
While in his heart he feels no violence

Laid on his humor and intelligence
When infant Science makes a pleasant face
And waves again that hollow toy, the Race;
No planetary trap where souls are wrought
For nothing but the sake of being caught
And sent again to nothing will attune
Itself to any key of any reason
Why man should hunger through another season
To find out why 'twere better late than soon
To go away and let the sun and moon
And all the silly stars illuminate
A place for creeping things,
And those that root and trumpet and have wings,
And herd and ruminate,
Or dive and flash and poise in rivers and seas,
Or by their loyal tails in lofty trees
Hang screeching lewd victorious derision
Of man's immortal vision.

Shall we, because Eternity records
Too vast an answer for the time-born words
We spell, whereof so many are dead that once
In our capricious lexicons
Were so alive and final, hear no more
The Word itself, the living word no man
Has ever spelt,
And few have ever felt
Without the fears and old surrenderings
And terrors that began
When Death let fall a feather from his wings
And humbled the first man?
Because the weight of our humility,
Wherefrom we gain
A little wisdom and much pain,
Falls here too sore and there too tedious,
Are we in anguish or complacency,
Not looking far enough ahead
To see by what mad couriers we are led
Along the roads of the ridiculous,
To pity ourselves and laugh at faith

And while we curse life bear it?
And if we see the soul's dead end in death,
Are we to fear it?
What folly is here that has not yet a name
Unless we say outright that we are liars?
What have we seen beyond our sunset fires
That lights again the way by which we came?
Why pay we such a price, and one we give
So clamoringly, for each racked empty day
That leads one more last human hope away,
As quiet fiends would lead past our crazed eyes
Our children to an unseen sacrifice?
If after all that we have lived and thought,
All comes to Nought, —
If there be nothing after Now,
And we be nothing anyhow,
And we know that, — why live?
'Twere sure but weaklings' vain distress
To suffer dungeons where so many doors
Will open on the cold eternal shores
That look sheer down
To the dark tideless floods of Nothingness
Where all who know may drown.

This text was first published in 1897, and this edition is a copy of a 1905 printing of the 1897 edition.

Index of First Lines

A

A melancholy face Charles Carville had, 37
A vanished house that for an hour I knew 149
Ah, — shuddering men that falter and shrink so 31
All you that are enamored of my name 103
Alone, remote, nor witting where I went, 49
Although I saw before me there the face 144
As eons of incalculable strife 82
As long as Fame's imperious music rings 10
As often as he let himself be seen 145
As often as we thought of her, 91
As we the withered ferns 16
At first I thought there was a superfine 43

B

"Be calm? And was I frantic? 179
Because he puts the compromising chart 32
Because he was a butcher and thereby 48
Between me and the sunset, like a dome 232
Blessed with a joy that only she 178
By what serene malevolence of names 211

C

Cliff Klingenhagen had me in to dine 36
Come away! come away! there's a frost along the ma 72
Confused, he found her lavishing feminine 159
Could he have made Priscilla share 224

D

Dark hills at evening in the west, 93
"Dear brother, dearest friend, when I am dead, 46
Dear friends, reproach me not for what I do, 27
"Do I hear them? Yes, I hear the children singing 125
Down by the flash of the restless water 13

F

Faint white pillars that seem to fade 222

For those that never know the light, 7
Friendless and faint, with martyred steps and slow 26

G

Give him the darkest inch your shelf allows, 52
Go to the western gate, Luke Havergal, — 22

H

Hamilton, if he rides you down, remember 107
He took a frayed hat from his head, 156
Herodion, Apelles, Amplias, 94

I

I cannot find my way: there is no star 53
I did not think that I should find them there 42
I found a torrent falling in a glen 84
I heard one who said: "Verily, 182
I met him, as one meets a ghost or two, 205
I pray you not, Leuconoe, to pore 47
I saw by looking in his eyes 89
If ever I am old, and all alone, 54
In dreams I crossed a barren land, 15
In Tilbury Town did Old King Cole 189

J

Just as I wonder at the twofold screen 40

L

Long warned of many terrors more severe 213
Look you, Dominie; look you, and listen! 59

M

My northern pines are good enough for me, 39

N

No longer torn by what she knows 218
"No, Mary, there was nothing — not a word. 165
No matter why, nor whence, nor when she came, 28
No sound of any storm that shakes 187
Not by the grief that stuns and overwhelms 25
Now in a thought, now in a shadowed word, 85
Now you have read them all; or if not all, 146

O

Observant of the way she told 106
Oh for a poet — for a beacon bright 51
Old Archibald, in his eternal chair, 124
Once there was a cabin here, and once there was a 186
Once, when I wandered in the woods alone, 30

S

She fears him, and will always ask 203
She'd look upon us, if she could, 215
Since Persia fell at Marathon, 20
Since you remember Nimmo, and arrive 153
Slowly I smoke and hug my knee, 14
So little have you seen of what awaits 104
Some are the brothers of all humankind, 11
Strange that I did not know him then, 12
Sweeping the chords of Hellas with firm hand, 29

T

"Tell me what you're doing over here, John Gorham, 184
Ten years together without yet a cloud, 142
The day was here when it was his to know 143
The Dead Village 38
The ghost of Ninon would be sorry now 212
The man Flammonde, from God knows where, 174
The man who cloaked his bitterness within 45
The master and the slave go hand in hand, 55
The master-songs are ended, and the man 69
The miller's wife had waited long, 92
There be two men of all mankind 19
There is a drear and lonely tract of hell 58
There is a fenceless garden overgrown 35
There were faces to remember in the Valley of the 86
They are all gone away, 23
Think not, because I wonder where you fled, 214
Though for your sake I would not have you now 117
Time was when his half million drew 228
To get at the eternal strength of things, 74
To the lore of no manner of men 221
Two men came out of Shannon's having known 139

U

Unyielding in the pride of his defiance, 105

Up from the street and the crowds that went, 17

V

Vengeful across the cold November moors, 33

W

"We are false and evanescent, and aware of our dec 123
We told of him as one who should have soared 141
We were all boys, and three of us were friends; 83
Well, Bokardo, here we are; 229
"When he was here alive, Eileen, 222
When he, who is the unforgiven, 209
When we can all so excellently give 57
Whenever I go by there nowadays 50
Whenever Richard Cory went down town, 24
Where a faint light shines alone, 216
"Where are you going to-night, to-night, — 21
"Whether all towns and all who live in them 130
"Why am I not myself these many days, 162
Why do you dig like long-clawed scavengers 56
With searching feet, through dark circuitous ways, 44
Withal a meagre man was Aaron Stark 34

Y

Ye gods that have a home beyond the world, 70
You are a friend then, as I make it out, 192
You that in vain would front the coming order 163